THEY NEVER COME BACK

THEY NEVER COME BACK

A Story of Undocumented Workers from Mexico

FRANS J. SCHRYER

ILR PRESS
AN IMPRINT OF
CORNELL UNIVERSITY PRESS
ITHACA AND LONDON

First published 2014 by Cornell University Press
First printing, Cornell Paperbacks, 2014
Printed in the United States of America

Library of Congress Cataloging-in-Publication Data

Schryer, Frans J., author.
   They never come back : a story of undocumented workers from Mexico /
Frans J. Schryer.
      pages cm
   Includes bibliographical references.
   ISBN 978-0-8014-5314-4 (cloth : alk. paper)
   ISBN 978-0-8014-7961-8 (pbk. : alk. paper)
   1. Foreign workers, Mexican—United States—Social conditions.
2. Foreign workers, Mexican—United States—Economic conditions.
3. Illegal aliens—United States—Social conditions. 4. Illegal aliens—
United States—Economic conditions. I. Title.
   HD8081.M6S36   2014
   331.6'2720973—dc23   2014012346

Cornell University Press strives to use environmentally responsible
suppliers and materials to the fullest extent possible in the publishing
of its books. Such materials include vegetable-based, low-VOC inks
and acid-free papers that are recycled, totally chlorine-free, or partly
composed of nonwood fibers. For further information, visit
our website at www.cornellpress.cornell.edu.

Cloth printing   10 9 8 7 6 5 4 3 2 1
Paperback printing   10 9 8 7 6 5 4 3 2 1

CONTENTS

Preface

In February 2006 I was traveling in a crowded van snaking its way along a dusty, potholed dirt road in the state of Guerrero, Mexico. The van serves as a small bus that takes people back and forth between the city of Iguala and one of the smaller towns whose inhabitants do their shopping and run errands there. I sat between two men and a woman sharing a narrow bench. Everyone spoke Nahuatl, the language used in that part of Guerrero. I struck up a conversation with the young man sitting on my left and found out that his parents had taken him and several of their other children with them to Houston, Texas, several years earlier. He switched to Spanish, then English, telling me he had recently come back from northern Mexico to make sure that his mother made it safely back across the border after a short visit to their hometown. The son planned to stay a bit longer before returning to the United States. This young man also told me the person who had most helped him learn English was a retired teacher in Houston, and he asked me for my e-mail address to give to her. It turns out that the teacher, who writes juvenile fiction, was interested in the native people of Mexico, a topic on which I have considerable expertise.

I corresponded with her and a year later stayed at her house during my first trip to the United States to start doing research on undocumented workers. My experience in that van is typical of the work done by anthropologists whose investigations sometimes lead us in unexpected directions.

In today's increasingly interconnected world, it does not make much sense to study migration by looking only at people in their place of origin, or conversely, their place of destination. By simultaneously doing fieldwork in the United States and in Mexico, I discovered that I could sometimes find out more about a town in Mexico from an interview with someone living in an apartment in a large urban center in the United States; likewise, I learned as much about the immigration experience from interviewing former migrants now living in Mexico as I did from talking to migrants in their homes and places of work north of the border. Talking to people on both sides of the U.S.-Mexico border enabled me to identify the hopes and dreams, as well as the disappointments and anxieties, of both undocumented workers and those they left behind.

In writing about undocumented workers, I want to give readers a good sense of what life is like for those who make it across the border. My goal is to provide American citizens, including those of Mexican descent, with a better understanding of undocumented migrants and the contribution undocumented workers make to the American economy. My hope is to illuminate not only the situation of undocumented migrants but also the urgent need to change the current system of immigration that is just not working. The focal point of this book is the sending communities. The existing literature usually provides more information on Mexican immigrants working and living in the United States than on the hometowns of those immigrants. My study will do the opposite. Previous research in Mexico and my knowledge of Nahuatl enables me to provide new insights into the impact of migration on sending communities and the emergence of new attitudes among those left behind. At the same time I provide ample coverage of the experiences and feelings of undocumented workers.

Until now, I have written books and journal articles for specialists in the field, presenting complex ideas using abstract, technical language. In contrast, this book is an example of public anthropology, which presents research results to a broader audience with the intention of contributing to public discussions on policy. I believe that the research of scholars and the implications of that research can be—and should be—explained in a way that is both thought-provoking and understandable to those without advanced academic degrees.

INTRODUCTION

Millions of undocumented Mexicans living in the United States feel boxed in. They might want to attend weddings in their hometowns or spend time with dying grandparents; but they need to keep their jobs and face increasing risks if they leave and then reenter. Consequently, few go back and forth anymore. These workers face additional challenges since it is now almost impossible for them to obtain a work permit or even identity documents. Consequently, to obtain work they have to acquire false documents or use the names of friends or relatives with valid Social Security numbers or work permits. Many cannot get or renew a driver's license yet they need to drive as part of their job or to find work. So they drive without a license. They do not like living this lie, but what other choices do they have?

The influx of undocumented workers is a consequence of the economic integration of the United States, Canada, and Mexico. The same McDonald's restaurants and other fast-food chains are found in each county. The major car makers have assembly plants all over the continent. Several large Mexican firms now do as much business in some parts of the United States as they do at home. Nowadays you are as likely to find an Avon lady or someone selling Amway products in a small town in southern Mexico as in Toronto or in downtown Los Angeles. You will see the same kind of iPods or cell phones wherever you go. The greater ease of circulation of goods and capital, especially after the implementation of the 1994 North American Free Trade Agreement (NAFTA), alongside further restriction on the movement of workers across borders, is a contradiction. An increase of undocumented workers, notwithstanding an agreement to reduce the need for Mexicans to find work in the United States, is another contradiction. Before the turn of the century Mexican men made frequent trips back home to visit their families, and mothers raised their children in Mexico. Today women are joining their husbands in the United States and young couples are migrating together, resulting in an increase in children born in the United States. Such children automatically become American citizens yet any brothers or sisters born in Mexico are aliens. Such alien offspring are Mexican citizens who will not learn about Mexican history; likewise children born in the U.S., but whose parents were forced to return to Mexico when they were still young, will grow up not knowing English or American history. All these contradictions are the outcome of a dysfunctional and hypocritical immigration policy.

Imagine if you found out that you are a Mexican when you thought you were an American. Imagine if you had no other choice but to move to a neighboring country as the only way to make a decent living, and then you are cut off from your family even though the place where they live is not that far away. Imagine if you had to make the choice between going back home to attend your father's funeral or keeping the job you need to support your children. Imagine going to a bus terminal after being away from your hometown for twenty years and realizing only after two hours that the stranger pacing back and forth is actually your father who is supposed to meet you and bring you and your baby back to the place you were born.

This book tells the stories of undocumented migrant workers, as well as the people they leave behind, using as an example people from the Alto Balsas region in the Mexican state of Guerrero. This part of Mexico is a good example to use because the proportion of migrants to the United States who are undocumented is very high, possibly over 90 percent. These migrant workers experience the inconsistencies of U.S. immigration policy; their stories illustrate how the economic integration of the North American continent, which at the same time restricts the movement of labor, is mirrored in people's lives. Migrants from this part of Mexico started working en masse as undocumented laborers only about fifteen years ago. Hence their experiences better illustrate these contradictions than the stories of those who emigrated before 1990. The workers described in this book are also representative of a recent trend in migration from the southern half of Mexico, where many people speak an indigenous language as their mother tongue.

Many books have been written about Mexican undocumented workers. Some writers emphasize the negative aspects of illegal migration by showing how such migrants are likely to be abused, and how they have few rights. Shannon Gleeson, who did research on immigrants' rights, focuses on the vulnerability of undocumented workers. She used the expression "those who work in the shadows." Others show the positive side by portraying migrants as resourceful agents, rather than passive victims. Judith Hellman points out that the women she interviewed enjoyed a new freedom from restrictive gender roles, while men learned new skills. Scholars and journalists have shown that these contrasting sides of migration are part of a single process of economic integration. The purpose of this book is not to replicate the studies that already exist. Rather, I will show how the contradictory nature of continental economic integration is reflected in the conflicted feelings and ambiguous situations of undocumented workers and those they leave behind.

I became aware of this feeling of ambivalence soon after I started doing research in the Mexican state of Guerrero whenever the topic of migration came up. All the children of Manuel, a widower I met in Mexico, now live in California. He told me in 2003: "They want me to come and live with them, but I don't want to spend the rest of my life in the U.S. My children send me money once in a while—a little, just enough for me to buy booze. That's what I do all day. I drink." He complained that his children never phone him. A year later I saw my landlady praying in front of a home altar. She pleaded with the Virgin of Guadalupe, Mexico's patron saint, to bring back her children; she had not heard from her sons for over six months. In talking with people throughout the Alto Balsas region, I kept hearing the expression, in the indigenous Nahuatl language, "*Xkaman waahloweh*" (they never come back). From their tone of voice, I sensed a feeling of frustration, loss, and disappointment. However, I was not particularly interested in the topic of migration when I first came across this expression.

During my first visit to rural Mexico, as a volunteer for a student project in the 1960s to help the poor, I became aware of how important it was for day laborers to have access to land so they could supplement their meager wages by growing corn. As a graduate student the research for my thesis in the Huasteca, a remote rural region located on the eastern side of Mexico, involved looking at how people make a living and their involvement in village politics. In the 1980s, now as an employed and practicing anthropologist, I examined an ongoing struggle over land and learned the Nahuatl language in order to interview peasant leaders. At that time no one I encountered in that part of Mexico even imagined the possibility of looking for work in the United States. When I subsequently chose another site for fieldwork, located further south and in Mexico's western half, I wanted to study the craft industry and the governance structure of indigenous communities.

The focus of my investigation in Guerrero changed in 2008 while conducting a survey in a town chosen for an in-depth study. Like many towns in the Alto Balsas region, its inhabitants move around a lot, making trips to other parts of Mexico as vendors or leaving home for extended periods to look for work, so it did not make much sense to go from house to house. Instead, I compiled a list of names and started looking for someone to go through that list. I approached Magdalena, a fifty-year-old woman living with her brother and sister-in-law. Magdalena had previously helped me with the transcription of taped interviews. Like many people her age, she once worked her family's corn plot and as a teenager she had made clay figurines. Today Magdalena is partly paralyzed and cannot walk as a result of an accident. She has never been in the United States, but she watches videos sent home by relatives and knows almost everyone from her village. Her answers to my questions opened up a window onto another world and inspired me to examine undocumented workers.

I gained further insights into international migration when I began making trips to several cities in the United States. A teenager, Delfino, told me:

> Living in the U.S. is very different. At home girls are not allowed to go to dances or parties without a chaperone. Here parents are not as strict, but the police—they're tough. If you make a mistake, you will end up in a big jail and you are likely to be deported. At home, we had this little jail, more like a room. If a man got drunk and hit someone, they would lock him up overnight. But the next day he would appear in front the mayor and say he was

sorry. He would give the village authorities money to buy mescal. Then they would let the man go—not in the U.S!

As I got to know more people from the Alto Balsas region working in the United States I encountered mixed feelings that were different from those I had found in Mexico. Delfino likes living in a big urban center in the United States and is well on his way to learning English. He appreciates the organized, orderly way things are done, although he resents the fact that his brother is going to get credit for the high school diploma he will obtain using Delfino's ID. Delfino finds it difficult to juggle different identities using other migrants' documents. He does not always know which name to use in which situation.

I detected ambivalence when I spoke to Paula, a young woman who left Mexico to discover what it would be like to live on her own, and to get to know her older brothers. She had not seen them since she was three years old. What she likes most about her new life is that she is no longer labeled an *ichpochlamantsin*, a term for a woman who is not yet married or living with a man. Paula is proud that she has figured out how to navigate the highways that crisscross the city where she is now living. But not everything is going as well as she had hoped. Paula began working in a restaurant in California while living with one of her brothers. He would not let her go to parties or drive on the freeway, so she moved to another state. A brother in Texas did not impose such restrictions and she got along well with him. He was supposed to get her a work permit. Paula looked up to him because he had worked his way up to become manager of two pizzerias. Yet in the end, Paula's brother did not succeed in getting her proper documentation. He is now back in Mexico after separating from his American wife. Today, three years later, Paula is still in Texas, living with a cousin and working a double shift at a donut shop. She too has mixed feelings:

> I got my job as cashier because I went beyond high school and know how to use a cash register. I have picked up enough English to figure out what people are ordering; but sometimes drive-in customers come in because they are lost. They ask me for instructions on how to get to a certain place. I cannot help them. My boss complains that I am not learning English quickly enough, but I can hardly understand him. He is Chinese [he is actually

Korean]. And I don't like that I drive without a license and that I am using my aunt's Social Security number.

As I continued to talk to people on both sides of the border, I came to appreciate the close intertwining of people's lives. It became clear that everyone's well-being is dependent on the failures and successes of others. When there is less work in California, relatives at home receive fewer remittances. When artisans in Mexico can no longer find customers, they too will migrate; their relatives in the United States will have to make room for more newcomers.

Almost all of the migrants from the Alto Balsas are undocumented workers, and their experiences have been a mixed blessing. Yet they continue to work in the supermarkets, construction sites, offices, and landscaping centers of American cities. Employers continue to hire them, knowing full well, or not wanting to know, that their workers are using false Social Security numbers or do not have green cards. I learned that the owner of a restaurant chain, who was levied a hefty fine for hiring undocumented Mexican workers, sold off half of his restaurants as franchises to entrepreneurs who had just emigrated from Cambodia. The new owners, in turn, hired these same workers. Employers need migrants willing to accept jobs many Americans are no longer willing to do on a permanent basis. Native-born Americans also work as busboys or dishwashers in restaurants, clean hotel rooms or put shingles on roofs, but they are more likely to quit because they prefer jobs with better pay and social benefits; many would rather go back to school to undergo training to enter more lucrative trades.

Today boys and girls from the Alto Balsas want to work in the United States as soon as they finish school because, until recently, the strategy of entering the United States as an undocumented worker paid off. There are no jobs in their home region and there is no future in growing corn in small plots on marginal land. Older family members who used to make a decent living selling crafts tell their children that tourists are no longer buying. At the same time, young people don't want to continue their studies in Mexico to become teachers, accountants, or lawyers, the way the children of better-off families used to do twenty years ago. They see how well migrants have done, how those who come back for a visit have the latest model cars. They know that in Mexico a nurse or a teacher, after years of study, will earn less than someone doing yard work or shelving groceries in

Los Angeles, Atlanta, or Houston. Young people continue trying to cross the border, no matter the cost or risks, and regardless of the likelihood that they will succeed. Those who have already been in the United States want to go again, and those currently there hope that with the right contacts and enough effort it might still be possible to obtain a green card.

In 1986 Congress passed a law making it possible for migrants who entered Mexico prior to 1982 to become legalized. At that time some people from several towns in the Alto Balsas got their papers, and at least forty of them are now American citizens. Those who have proper documents can drive back to Mexico to attend hometown festivals and visit family. But those cases are rare; I can think of only four other people who have since obtained work permits. If a young person is lucky enough to have an uncle who is "legal," and who also has the same surname, it might be possible to enter the United States without paying a lot of money. That uncle will have to drive to the border and pretend to be the father, but once in the United States that "son" or "daughter" will still have to buy false papers. Undocumented migrants, who live in a perpetual state of insecurity, represent a shadowy part of American society.

Organization of the Book and Research Overview

Chapter 1 provides an overview of the Alto Balsas as the background for my case study, placing this region into the broader context of the social and economic development of Mexico, with additional comments on the nature of Mexican race and ethnic relations. Chapter 2 focuses on the craft production that provided the inhabitants of the Alto Balsas with a viable alternative to migrant labor from around 1950 to the mid-eighties. This and the following ten chapters include direct quotes as a way of allowing both undocumented migrants and those who have never or seldom left Mexico to tell their stories. Some people will be heard only once, while others will come back again and again as I trace their personal lives and their careers on both sides of the border. For example, Delfino, the young man in the van mentioned in the preface, makes his next appearance in chapter 9. I follow the stories of other migrants who used to go back and forth between Mexico and the United States. Many of these chapters shift between Mexico and the United States to highlight the connections between migrants and those they leave behind. The emphasis in chapters 3 and 4 is on the impact of migrant labor on life in the sending communities, while chapters 6 to 8 provide insights into the world of work, including relations between migrant workers and their employers. The stories in those chapters illustrate the challenges and opportunities, as well as the hardships, faced by undocumented workers. I try to strike a balance between successes and failures by including examples of errors and mistakes, as well as acts of kindness. Deportations are the subject of chapter 10, and chapter 11 shows how the customs and form of governance typical of indigenous communities shape the lives of migrants. Chapter 12 examines the differences between various categories of young people, depending on their legal, status, how long they have been in the United States, as well as whether or not they have gone back to Mexico. In chapter 13, which provides an overview of the quandaries faced by migrant families, I draw more on the research of other scholars and we hear less from the migrants themselves. In this final chapter, I return to the theme of the broken system of immigration as a way of linking my case study to ongoing discussions on public policy.

Because my book is not specifically geared to an academic readership, I do not use footnotes, with one exception in this chapter. None of the chapters, even those that draw on secondary sources, include bibliographical references, although I do mention the names of specific researchers. Readers who want to know who published the books consulted, with titles and dates of publication, can consult a final section called "Suggested Readings and References."

It is customary for an author to add some comments on how and when the research for an ethnography was carried out. In my case, I spent the bulk of my time in the Alto Balsas region of Guerrero, with each trip lasting anywhere from several weeks to several months, adding up to well over a year. That does not include additional short visits to Chilpancingo, the state capital, the city of Iguala, or other parts of Mexico. (I do not consider the one-week vacations I sometimes take in Mexico with my wife as part of my research, although on two occasions I did take notes on short conversations with craft vendors on the island of Cozumel and the coast of Nayarit.) All this took place during a period of over a decade, from 2001 until 2013. I carried out a survey in one of the bigger towns of the Alto Balsas region to obtain basic demographic data plus information on land use and migration. Starting in 2011, two years after I moved to Toronto, I started conducting interviews once a week from my home office with several people in that same town in the Alto Balsas. Those phone interviews, which include questions about recent deaths and marriages, and who has since come back to Mexico, were still being done at the time I was putting the finishing touches on the final version of this book.

I did not spend as much time in the United States as I did in Mexico, nor had I done previous fieldwork there. Eight visits to three urban centers in the United States, lasting from one to three weeks each, added up to about three months over the course of the last five years. During all but two of my trips, I stayed in the homes of undocumented workers. I had already met some people in Mexico, while others were completely new contacts. I also visited several workplaces in the United States. During my visits to the United States, I spoke to people from four different towns in Guerrero, although I concentrated on migrants from the town where I did my survey. In each city, one person helped me figure out who now works there or who lived there but has since gone back to Mexico or moved to another American city. I wanted to make sure that the information I had already obtained in my Mexico survey was accurate, and to get an idea of the number of U.S.-born children. By the time I finished this book I had information on 3,791 people.

I did not conduct fieldwork in the regions on opposite sides of the border between the United States and Mexico, nor did I ever accompany anyone from Guerrero across the border; but enough men and women have told me about their experiences of crossing the border to allow me to at least touch on this aspect of their migration experience in chapter 5. To obtain a more complete picture of indigenous migrants from other Mexican regions in the United States, I drew on the work of other scholars. My book likewise brings in the findings and insights of researchers who specialize in international immigration and immigration policy. My contribution is to put a human face on the facts and figures, as well as on the arguments presented in other studies.

Finally, I want to alert readers that my book does not dwell on the obvious unfairness of undocumented workers not being paid overtime and not getting sick leave or vacation pay. The aim of this book is not to make the argument that people are unable to earn enough money or that they are being exploited, but rather to show that they are living in a state of ongoing uncertainty. The real tragedy is that so many people will never be able to achieve their full potential. Undocumented Mexicans are perpetually kept waiting, hoping against hope that they might eventually become "legal." They do not know what the future holds in store for them. They can never feel at home. That feeling of insecurity might be the reason so many people want to use their savings to build a house in Mexico, even if they know deep down in their hearts they might never live in that house. Similarly, it is ironic that I cannot provide the names of real places and real people.[1] I do this to protect my informants, even though they would have preferred for readers to know who they are; the way I write about migrants is a reflection of the contradictions inherent in an economic system that makes illegal the work that is needed to make the system work.

---

1. The stories in this book are based on what real people have told me, but their names have been changed to mask identities. Every pseudonym corresponds to a different person. In the cases of place names, I occasionally used the real names of cities in the United States and towns in Mexico, but I have also switched around the name of places or used deliberately vague phrases such as "hometown." All references to states (California, Guerrero, Texas) are real.

1

What Happened to the Mexican Miracle?

Many tourists visiting Mexico are shocked when they see shantytowns, grown men shining shoes, and small boys darting in and out of traffic to clean windshields at traffic lights. But poverty or prosperity is relative. Around 1990, when I showed a student from mainland China a photograph of a village in one of the regions where I was conducting fieldwork, he said, "Mexico must be a rich country; those people seem well-off compared to China's countryside." Indeed, overall standards of living have risen over the past fifty years throughout Mexico. In the region where I did my research, older people tell me they used to be much poorer. When I asked them how their lives today differ from the past, they kept on telling me that they used to suffer a lot:

> When we were growing up we did not wear shoes, but sandals with soles made from used car tires. There was no electricity and we used candles. There were no roads. Women got up at four in the morning to fetch water at springs that often ran dry. We lived in thatched or palm-roofed huts

without chimneys, so the smoke from cooking hearths would sting our eyes. Women used to grind their cornmeal by hand. Our hair was full of lice, and we were bitten by bedbugs.

People told me that it was impossible to meet their needs solely by growing corn. Most men worked as day laborers in neighboring regions to earn money to buy salt, a new hat, or cotton cloth for making clothes. The only luxuries were Mexican hot chocolate or *pan dulce* (sweetbread) for special occasions. No one drank bottled beer or sodas. Most towns did not have schools. Such living conditions were identical to what I observed in the 1960s as a student volunteer in another part of Mexico. Both regions were left behind in the economic growth following World War II. But since then both regions have seen a rise in living standards and better public services.

Nowadays there are elementary schools in every village and most houses are on the electrical grid. Many towns have a health clinic. The problem is that there are few opportunities to get ahead, even by moving to another part of Mexico. This is the main reason young people opt to go to the United States. None speak or understand English, but they have all gone to school where they learned Spanish. These same young migrants are familiar with the terrain of their place of origin. Each mountainside or ravine where they fetched water for their family donkey, or helped to transplant chili plants while growing up, has its own name: Lamasapotitlan, Wei Tlahli, Itsahchiampoyoh, Tekorral, Tepeyekapitstle.

The History of the Alto Balsas

The Alto, or Upper, Balsas, named after a section of the Balsas River, consists of eighteen towns located on both sides of that river. This area was once part of the pre-Columbian region of Mesoamerica, prior to the Spanish conquest, and corresponds to the central and southern portions of what is today Mexico plus most of Central America. The best known groups in this region were the Mayans and the Aztecs, whose rulers used sophisticated calendars and built pyramids. The language of the Aztecs, or Meshica, from which the word Mexico is derived, is still spoken today in the Alto Balsas. It is called Nahuatl, and people who speak it are referred to as Nahuas. Yet they do not identify themselves as Nahuas, and most of them do not call their language by that name. They will tell you they speak Mexicano, which actually means they do not speak Spanish as their home language! Children do not learn about their own region's history when they go to school to learn how to speak and read Spanish.

Historians have discovered that, prior to the Spanish conquest, people in the Alto Balsas paid tribute to rulers who lived in Tenochtitlan, the Aztec capital that was then larger than any European city, including Madrid. I will not dwell on the tragic story of how Spanish conquerors destroyed most of Tenochtitlan, now known as Mexico City. These new rulers imposed the Roman Catholic branch of Christianity, which did not fully take root. Even today indigenous Mexicans practice a form of folk Catholicism with many pre-Columbian elements. During the three hundred years when Mexico was under Spanish colonial rule, intermarriage resulted in the formation of a new social group called mestizos. Today Spanish-speaking Mexicans consider themselves to be mestizos, as opposed to *indígenas*, which refers to those who speak an indigenous language. Most Americans would not be aware of such distinctions among the Mexican migrants who live in their midst.

By the eighteenth century Mexico, then called New Spain, was the envy of the world; its mines produced gold and silver and large landed estates called haciendas rivaled the properties owned by the European aristocracy. New Spain was a key component of a commercial empire. Spanish galleons moved goods from the Orient to Europe via Mexico; cargo brought on board in the Philippines was unloaded in Acapulco on Mexico's Pacific coast to the south of Alto Balsas. There spices and silk were put on the backs of mules to be driven to the port of Veracruz located on Mexico's Atlantic coast, and then again loaded up for another sea journey. The Nahua muleteers who transported these goods during the first stage of the overland journey were a vital link in a global economy. Given the dry nature of their terrain, which only allows one maize crop per year, the inhabitants of the Alto Balsas were itinerant traders during the dry season. Apart from transporting goods for wealthy Spanish merchants, they struck out on their own; they transported dried food on the backs of donkeys, to be exchanged for salt on the coast. These traders sold the salt in the highland regions of northern Guerrero. Nahuas also knew how to get people and goods across the turbulent Balsas River on rafts. This tradition of traveling and trading helped them to later adapt to new forms of making a livelihood; today people frequently travel back and forth between their home region and other parts of Mexico. By 1960 some Nahuas were going back and forth to the United States.

For most Mexicans today, working in the United States is an attractive alternative to staying in Mexico, but this was not always the case. During the colonial era, the French, English, and Dutch colonists in what are now the United States and Canada were poor cousins in comparison to the Spanish colonists and their descendants in New Spain. This was still true when the English colonies that became the United States of America declared independence in 1776. By 1870 a then much larger American republic was well on its way to becoming a powerful nation. But people then living in the Alto Balsas would not even have heard of the United States of America. Many of them were not even aware that they were citizens of a county called Mexico.

The Painful Emergence of a Mexican Nation

Mexico became an independent country early in the nineteenth century, but its new rulers were the same people of Spanish descent who were its landowners, merchants, and professionals then and throughout the colonial era. Mexico's colonial rulers had used Nahuatl in addition to Spanish for court cases, land records, and commercial transactions in many regions. Ironically, Mexican independence in 1821 meant the adoption of Spanish as the only official language; Nahuatl became an oral language only. Between Mexico's independence and today, the proportion of Mexicans speaking Nahuatl and other local languages gradually declined, yet today 15 percent of Mexico's population still speak an indigenous language, of which there are more than fifty. Most people born in the Alto Balsas still speak Nahuatl at home, even in downtown Los Angeles, Houston, and in the suburbs of Atlanta.

The first half of the nineteenth century was a period of rapid decline, when Mexico was engulfed with political infighting between Liberals and Conservatives, as in the rest of Latin America. Mexico also lost its independence for a while, in 1863, when foreign forces occupied Mexico City. The French government imposed an Austrian emperor, but his short-lived rule ended with his execution by a firing squad after Liberal forces defeated the French army. The victorious Liberals abolished old forms of land ownership, including the Catholic Church's extensive landholdings. Anyone who has attended school in Mexico knows the national history sketched out so far; all Mexicans, including undocumented workers from the Alto Balsas region now living in the United States, would recognize the name Benito Juarez, a prominent nineteenth-century Liberal lawyer and national president. They know he was a Zapotec Indian.

Land reforms implemented during the last quarter of the nineteenth century had a disastrous impact on many towns in Mexico whose communally owned land had remained intact throughout the colonial era. Such towns, treated as Indian republics, once had their own elected officials as part of a form of limited self-rule during the colonial era. The Mexican state decided to privatize all remaining communal village lands, resulting in an even greater concentration of land ownership in the hands of large landowners. Nevertheless, some indigenous towns found ways to prevent their land from passing into the hands of outsiders. This was the case for towns in the Alto Balsas. In the case of Ahuehuepan, a group of better-off villagers even managed to buy additional land. The Liberals also wanted to make schooling available to everyone as a way of promoting democracy, yet a large proportion of Mexico's population did not speak Spanish. In the Alto Balsas only a handful of people could read and write Spanish, even as late as 1970.

The older Nahua migrants today working in the United States have witnessed huge changes during their lifetime, including the introduction of schools. However, compulsory education and other recent developments are the culmination of a long process of urbanization and industrialization set in motion over 150 years ago as a result of the policies implemented during the reign of Porfirio Díaz. Díaz was first elected president of Mexico in 1877 and ruled with an iron fist for several decades. He and his entourage of advisers promoted foreign investment, resulting in the construction of a large network of railroads and large-scale, semi-industrialized, agricultural enterprises. The new railways transported sugar cane, minerals, and other products northward to the United States. But uneven economic development and a lack of democracy resulted in the outbreak of ten years of civil war known as the Mexican Revolution. The Revolution, which started in 1910, led to widespread destruction, and shattered the economy. In the Alto Balsas older people, whose parents witnessed these events, tell horror stories; girls hid in caves so that they would not be raped, and soldiers took whatever food was available, and ordered older women to prepare large quantities of tortillas. A few men in each town joined one or another of the revolutionary bands, but not because they had lost land. The Nahua towns still had their original communal lands, and prosperous families owned cattle, including oxen used as plough animals. Those animals disappeared and commerce was disrupted. It took several decades to recover from this social upheaval. The Mexican Revolution is firmly entrenched in the memory of Mexicans who learn about its heroes and villains when they attend school. The name of one of those heroes, Emiliano Zapata, is a powerful political symbol, as illustrated by the 1994 Zapatista uprising in Chiapas in southern Mexico.

Between the 1920s and the year 2000 Mexico was a de-facto one-party state, with several changes in the name of what became the PRI (Institutional Revolutionary Party). During this period, the country underwent many social, political, and economic changes. During the twenties and thirties, the Mexican state gradually reestablished centralized control after adopting a new constitution hammered out among competing factions. Officially, the new state was supposed to introduce social reforms and protect the rights of workers, but there was a huge gap between what was written in the constitution and what actually happened on the ground. One-party rule and limited reforms went hand in hand with political stability, and the national economy slowly recovered. However, not everyone benefited. For example, farmers in the Alto Balsas were still able to supplement their income through the salt trade but this became more difficult with the construction of a highway from Mexico City to Acapulco. Truckers now traveled to the coast to bring back salt, and the Mexican government placed restrictions on muleteers after 1931, the same year that saw the completion of an unpaved highway that passed through the town of Xalitla at the western edge of the Alto Balsas. People now went by foot or donkey to Xalitla to board vehicles to reach a large market in the city of Iguala. Others used this route to find work in the dry season in the more fertile fields of the valley of Iguala. Men worked for part of the year in small sugar cane mills or for a lumber mill, and young women from several towns used this same road to travel by bus to Mexico City to work as maids. Others became seasonal agricultural laborers in the nearby state of Morelos. At the national level, land ownership continued to be highly unequal, despite the promises of the Revolution to better the lot of the landless peasants.

The widespread redistribution of land did not happen until after the election of Lázaro Cárdenas in 1934, when the government in power swung further to the left, in both words and deeds. The acceleration of land reform meant that a substantial number of landless peasants gained access to arable land and even people in regions like the Alto Balsas got additional land. Cardenas also expropriated foreign oil companies to create PEMEX, the national oil consortium. The name Cárdenas and the political movement and ideology associated with his name (Cardenismo) became an influential stream in Mexican politics. Over the next few decades this political current evolved into a movement of opposition to the one-party rule of the PRI, the same party to which many members of that oppositional movement once belonged. Indeed, the founder of the main leftist party today, the PRD (Party of the Democratic Revolution), is Cuauhtémoc Cárdenas, son of the man who nationalized the Mexican oil industry. This new political party has won the governorship of the state of Guerrero on several occasions, and ongoing electoral competition between the PRD and the old PRI is one of the defining features of local politics in the Alto Balsas region today.

Although the name Cárdenas is associated with socialism in Mexico, his policies as president actually promoted the further development of industrial capitalism, and facilitated the creation of privately owned commercial farms. The Mexican state also initiated a process of economic development based on high tariffs on imported goods to stimulate the creation of Mexican-owned factories. Other Latin American countries implemented a similar policy, known as import substitution. In Mexico, the subsequent growth of manufacturing and construction, starting in 1940, transformed the national economy. This was the start of what political scientists and economists called the Mexican miracle. Between 1945 and 1980 Mexico became an increasingly more industrialized and urbanized nation. Traditional subsistence agriculture became less important and poor rural inhabitants converged on their capital, Mexico City, which became what was at that time the largest city in the world.

The Mexican miracle had its winners and losers. Guerrero continued to be one of the poorest states, but within that state the Alto Balsas region experienced a short-lived boom, partly as a result of the paving of the highway from Mexico City to Acapulco, at a time when the Mexican government was promoting tourism. American tourists were now able to drive to places such as Taxco and Acapulco. It did not take long for people in the Alto Balsas to realize that one could earn more money selling crafts to tourists than by working for wages. Craft production throughout Mexico expanded rapidly because of the emergence of a more prosperous middle class, including professionals and owners of small businesses who could afford to travel to beach resorts on the Pacific coast. They had the disposable income to stay longer and to buy the handicrafts at the same time that international tourism was expanding. What makes the Alto Balsas unique is that most of the Nahuas sold and many still sell these crafts directly to tourists, without middlemen. Consequently, most people no longer had to work as hired hands in neighboring regions. But the craft boom did not last long, as we shall see in chapter 2.

The economic growth associated with the Mexican miracle slowed down and the government incurred huge debts. To stave off incipient unrest in the countryside, the Mexican state, under President Luis Echeverria in the 1970s, resurrected land reform, and started providing credit to corn farmers and small coffee producers to stimulate rural development. It could afford to do so because of the discovery of offshore oil, which enabled the government to finance its social programs. The Alto Balsas continued to see the expansion of schools, the introduction of electricity, and the building of new roads. Such improvements in infrastructure, combined with limited political reform, ensured continued political stability. However, Mexico's continued dependence on oil revenues, the failure to invest in better refining facilities, and continued subsidies for state enterprises resulted in a further deterioration of its economy. The end result was rampant inflation, culminating in the revaluation of the peso. Even the most successful Nahua craft vendors started to feel the pinch.

Starting in the 1970s, Mexico saw the gradual transformation of a nationalistic, state-led model of development into one emphasizing commercial ties with the United States, the first step toward continental integration. The first phase was the promotion of textile assembly plants in a free-trade zone near the border (called *maquiladores*), and the end of protective barriers for manufacturers. These measures averted an economic crisis but did not help such regions as Guerrero. The next logical step, following the new economic theory of neoliberalism, was the signing of the North American Free

Trade Agreement (NAFTA) in 1994. U.S. investment now flowed freely, as it had done under Porfirio Diaz. However, new jobs created by American investors were offset by the loss of jobs in the Mexican-owned companies that had once been protected by tariffs. Emigration increased, even though it became more and more difficult to cross the border, since the free trade agreement did not include the notion of a free labor market. The people who designed NAFTA thought that it would create enough jobs that Mexicans would want to stay home. Instead the level of migration to the United States, which had always acted as a safety valve when the Mexican economy could not provide enough jobs, increased very rapidly. In the Alto Balsas, the further erosion of the craft trade meant that its population became more dependent on other sources of income at a time when the jobs that were supposed to come with continental economic integration did not materialize.

The Border and International Migration

People from Mexico have been going to the United States for a long time, taking into account that the entire Southwest, including California, was part of Mexico until 1848. It is difficult to calculate the extent of emigration prior to the outbreak of the Mexican Revolution, because people, as well as goods, were constantly streaming back and forth along an open border. At the turn of the century, some people from the more populated central part of Mexico also started heading for the border regions, usually by rail. However, few Mexicans stayed on the American side of the border prior to 1910, until political refugees started moving to the United States during the Mexican Revolution. By 1920, Mexico's economy was still weak and people again started going back and forth across the border. However, it does not make much sense to talk about international migration from Mexico to the United States prior to that time because there was in effect no border control. People living on both sides of the Rio Grande moved back and forth, as if there was no border; at the same time most people in other parts of Mexico were not interested in leaving their homes. This situation changed when labor recruiters started arriving from the American Southwest. These recruiters, called *enganchadores*, moved south along the rail lines that reached the more populated western and central Mexican states. The word *enganche* means "hook"; the labor recruiters, who acted as loan sharks, offered to pay poor Mexican farmers advances to cover the cost of travel to the United States where they were guaranteed seasonal work in the burgeoning American economy. These recruiters did not go further south to areas such as the Alto Balsas, where no one even thought about the possibility of "going north." However, central and northern Mexico saw a massive exodus of people who soon constituted a significant proportion of the unskilled labor force in several key sectors of the American economy, especially in agriculture, construction, meatpacking plants, and railroad track maintenance.

The era of the *enganche* peaked in 1924, the same year that saw the creation of the U.S. Border Patrol. This era ended in 1929, just prior to the Great Depression. The Depression resulted in a high level of deportation of most Mexicans who had not already gone home voluntarily, including some people of Mexican descent who were American citizens. American business had first taken the initiative to import Mexican labor, but when that labor was no longer needed, the American government closed its border with Mexico until they again needed Mexican workers, such as in the 1940s and 1950s when a migrant program begun under President Franklin D. Roosevelt again provided work for Mexican farmworkers. This program, which coincided with the rapid urbanization of Mexico in the fifties, removed the pressures associated with the need for the Mexican economy to absorb an ever increasing number of people fleeing the countryside in search of work. A handful of men in the Alto Balsas took advantage of this program, but most people were still able to make a good living during the craft boom. The American bracero program (*brazo* means arm) lasted until 1965, but Mexicans nevertheless continued to cross the border at a time of high demand for Mexican labor in the United States. For the next twenty years a small number of agricultural workers still worked in the United States under a new kind of contract arrangement, but the bulk of migrants were undocumented. A bigger budget for border control resulted in numerous apprehensions of illegal migrants who were shipped back to Mexico after signing a voluntary departure order. Yet most migrants made numerous attempts to reenter and border officials often turned a blind eye. Some Mexicans decided to stay in the United States, but most undocumented workers simply went back and forth in what some writers label a revolving door system. The outcome was a de facto guest workers program that lasted well into the 1980s.

During this era of increasing migration, some people from the Alto Balsas started joining the stream of undocumented workers from other parts of the country. Initially, most of them did not distinguish between the U.S. and Mexican states close to the border; they were just going somewhere far away to earn some extra money, just like the braceros who had gone away earlier to work with what was referred to in the Alto Balsas as "the signature of the governor." They had every intention of coming back soon. For the first time men, as well as a few women, went to Los Angeles to work in clothing factories instead of working on American farms. Working in the United States now became an additional option for people who wanted to earn money to build better houses. Remittances also financed community projects. For example, one group of migrants working in California used part of their earnings to cover the cost of a new set of wooden benches for their hometown church. During the seventies and eighties, most migrants came from just a few towns (Xalitla, Maxela, and Ahuelican), but people from other towns also started crossing the border after the collapse of the Mexican peso in 1982. In the Alto Balsas, increasing competition among craft vendors and the increasing costs of art supplies made this form of generating income more difficult. Some people who had previously been artisans and vendors now also opted to work in the United States. The downturn in the Mexican economy likewise had a devastating impact on those people who had earlier moved to the national capital to work.

Ruben from Ahuelican is an example of someone from the Alto Balsas then living in Mexico City. Orphaned at age three, he grew up in the household of an uncle who saw the importance of children going to school to learn how to read and write. Ruben was a promising student with a dedicated teacher who helped him continue his studies in the city of Iguala, after attending the village school for three years. In Iguala he worked as a domestic servant in return for room and board. At age fifteen his uncle came to bring him back to Ahuelican to help him take care of his animals. Consequently Ruben did not go to high school, in Mexico City, until he was seventeen years old. There Ruben again worked as a domestic while studying to obtain a high school diploma. That is where he met Juana, a young woman from his hometown, whom we will meet later. She originally came to Mexico City to work as a maid.

When I met my wife, I was still living in the house where I worked as a male servant, and we stayed there for five years. All that time I was still finishing my high school courses, but I wanted to continue my studies to become an accountant. I took an entrance exam together with thousands of other students, at the UNAM, Mexico's national university, and was accepted. I studied there for two years but did not finish. I had only one year left.

Ruben dropped out of the university in 1985, when his first son was born. In the meantime he and Juana had already moved in with Ruben's older sister in another part of the city. Ruben worked for two years as a filing clerk in a textile factory that made sweaters, while attending night school in a private school to obtain a diploma in accounting. When he lost that job he started doing manual labor for a company that built sidewalks and cut sewer pipes. Ruben and Juana made occasional visits to attend festivals in his hometown, but they spent most of their time in Mexico City. In the meantime, a number of men from Ahuelican started working as undocumented workers in large supermarkets in the United States. Ruben's brother-in-law, at that time living in Texas, offered to help Ruben to pay for the cost of crossing the border as an undocumented worker. Ruben had just obtained his accounting diploma and thought he might be able to use it to get a white-collar job working in a state archive somewhere in Mexico. When he found out he would first have do a year of social service work without pay, he opted to emigrate; he had to earn money to support his family, so he had no other choice but to move to the United States. Initially, Juana stayed in Mexico City but she joined Ruben in 1992. Around this time the wives and other family members of migrant workers from Ahuelican stayed behind to continue to grow corn for their own consumption, with the help of day laborers who were paid with money sent back by those working in the United States.

Starting in the eighties people all over Mexico became undocumented workers and their arrival in the United States seemed to be spiraling out of control. In 1986, the U.S. Congress, during the presidency of Ronald Reagan, passed the Immigration Reform and Control Act that provided an amnesty for undocumented workers, but at the same time imposed stricter border controls. Suddenly 2.3 million undocumented migrants were eligible to be legalized. Workers who had been in the United States for at least five years were eligible to apply for work permits and could eventually become American citizens. Some men from a few towns in the Alto Balsas thus obtained the documents that enabled them to freely travel back and forth between the United States and Mexico. In the United States the rate of illegal migrants, as measured by the number of people apprehended at the border, dropped dramatically, but only for several years; by 1990 the rate of border crossings exceeded that of the preamnesty era. Austerity measures under President Salinas de Gortari provided even greater incentives for Mexicans to migrate. The existence of a network of social ties between Mexicans already in the United States and those at home made illegal border crossings easier, because friends and relatives in the United States could help new migrants figure out how to cross the border and get jobs. This was the case in the Alto Balsas, where networks established since the early days of limited migration now spread throughout the entire region.

In 1990, the Alto Balsas faced a challenge greater than the one posed by inflation and the need to cross the border to find work. The Mexican government, which continued its program of rapid modernization, albeit at a slower pace, decided to build a new hydroelectric dam that would have flooded a large portion of the Alto Balsas. They had done all of their planning without consulting any of the affected towns. It is not this book's purpose to cover the ensuing social movement culminating in the cancellation of the dam project in September 1992. Suffice it to say that this movement, which was entirely peaceful, was partly financed by migrants then living in California. It is worth noting that the leadership for resistance against the dam project came from a handful of professionals, including several Nahua anthropologists who were born and raised in the region. Indeed, they coined the group name "Nahuas of the Alto Balsas" now used by all anthropologists as well as by journalists. I use the name in this book, even though very few people in the region are familiar with this term.

By 1994 people from about half of the Alto Balsas towns were working and living in the United States. However, the pace of out-migration, this time from the whole region, picked up significantly only after the signing of an international agreement that was supposed to slow down the pace of migration. One year after NAFTA took effect Mexico also saw a massive devaluation of the peso. From that point on, families became increasingly dependent on remittances from migrants in the United States and people from every town in the region became undocumented workers. Fewer men and women ventured off to other parts of Mexico, although almost a third of the population continued to follow familiar routes to sell crafts. The population of the region was now scattered across both Mexico and the southern half of the United States.

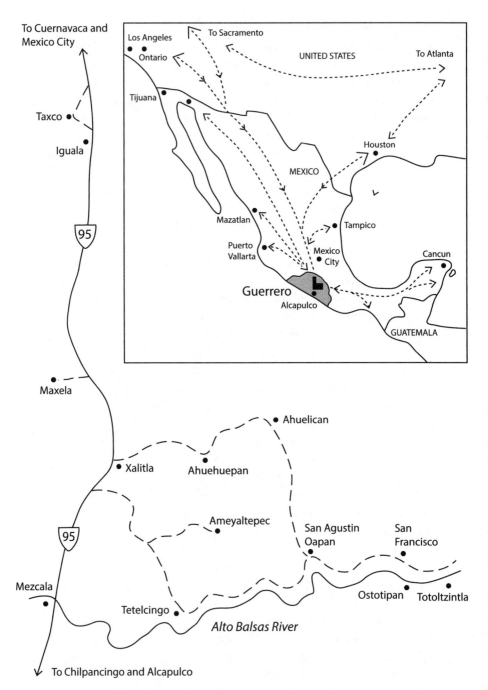

Origin and destination of migrants from the Alto Balsas region (Guerrero)

The Alto Balsas after NAFTA

Today it is becoming even more difficult to get jobs in both Mexico and the United States, yet consumerism is creating a demand to buy more and more things that used to be luxuries but are now considered to be necessities. Throughout North America more cell phones, blenders, and iPods are now available for lower prices, but the number of people who can no longer afford to buy what they need or want is also increasing, especially in Mexico. In 2005, a Nahua school teacher who lives in the same town as my local assistant Magdalena said to me:

> I told my oldest daughter that I wanted her to start helping us a bit because my salary as a teacher no longer allows me to support the whole family. Right now I am only making two thousand pesos (two hundred dollars) every two weeks. I would earn more but they are making deductions because of a previous loan. I could live on my regular salary if just my wife and I lived here. But Paula wants to buy expensive clothes in Iguala. She likes the latest fashions as shown on TV. She buys shoes that cost two hundred or three hundred pesos. She likes her cell phone and wants to buy a new one that she can use for making videos.

The teacher's daughter was unable to get a job in Mexico, so she went to the United States to look for work. There are many more jobs in the United States than in Mexico, even during periods of recession. Mexicans who do not have jobs can no longer make a living by growing corn if they live in the countryside, or by selling chewing gum or polishing shoes if they live in cities or bigger towns. Furthermore, the demand for crafts from vendors from the Alto Balsas has shrunk, and no longer provides a means of livelihood for all but the most experienced craft vendors with established clients.

In Mexico, dissatisfaction with the political status quo, combined with a further decline in the purchasing power of Mexican consumers, culminated in the defeat of the Institutional Revolutionary Party in 2000, marking the end of the policies associated with the regime that was initially responsible for the Mexican miracle. Yet despite some further growth in the Mexican economy, the number of people crossing the Mexican border kept increasing. This exodus did not abate until after the events of 9/11; yet Mexicans, including the vast majority of young people in the Alto Balsas, continue to look for work in the United States despite ever more sophisticated border control measures. The gap in wages and living standards between the two neighboring countries has not narrowed enough.

2

"STRUGGLING TO GET AHEAD"

In February 2009, my wife and I visited the coastal town of La Peñita, north of Puerto Vallarta, where we stayed in a bed and breakfast.
We were picked up by Pedro, a craft vendor whom I had met during
previous stays in Mexico. Pedro took us to Rincon de Huayabitos, a
nearby resort town that has a better beach and a good restaurant. He then
invited us to visit his second home in La Peñita and told us about his life
as a vendor:

> There are about seven hundred vendors here who sell to tourists. Thirty of
> us are from Ahuehuepan. There is a lot of competition, but the sun shines
> on all of us. For twenty years I walked back and forth to Huayabitos every
> day. During the day I still sell necklaces to people on the beach, carrying a
> display board around my neck. But on Thursdays I sell pottery and paint-
> ings at the market in La Peñita. In the evenings I set up a booth in Deca-
> maron, an all-inclusive hotel. Eight of us do that and we pay eighty pesos in
> rent for using that space.

Pedro's story illustrates the art and craft industry, which until recently enabled a third of the families of his hometown to make a decent living. However, the craft industry, once a success story, has undergone a gradual decline. The children of artisans have not succeeded in replicating their parents' careers. They too have ended up in the United States, where they no longer paint or carve.

The emergence of craft production in the Alto Balsas is a story in itself. Originally, craft production was mainly for home use: women made jars for holding water and pots for straining the lime water used to soak corn. Men made firecrackers used in religious celebrations, or burned wood to make charcoal. Some of these objects were sold or traded in neighboring towns. In the early fifties, young men in the town of Ameyaltepec started to experiment with painting designs on various surfaces, to create something to sell to outsiders. The most successful medium was a type of paper made from the bark of the *amate* tree, once used by the Aztecs. A painting on this bark paper is also called an amate. For several years only three families were involved in painting amates on commission, but gradually craft production spread throughout the community. Amate painting was also adopted in Oapan and other villages where new styles were developed. Other forms of craft production were also initiated or invented; some villages specialized in making masks, others in carving wooden figurines or decorating gourds, clay ashtrays, and bowls. Artisans in Ahuehuepan made clay necklaces and later began using the same designs that first appeared on amates when painting clayware and carved wooden fish that were strung together to create mobiles.

The history of the craft industry of the Alto Balsas is unique because the majority of artisans used to market their own products, making frequent trips to other parts of Mexico to sell directly to consumers. Initially this was tough going; artisans did not have permits, so what they wanted to sell was confiscated by the police. An artisan and vendor from Oapan who now spends most of his time in downtown Cuernavaca recalled how it was not easy for him and other vendors:

> I first came here to sell by myself, like other vendors. I did that for two years, until we came together. There were a lot of inspectors who used to just take our merchandise and they did not give it back to us. We were constantly being harassed so we formed an association. It was all settled about

twenty-three years ago, and they can no longer get rid of us. However, we still do not have our own market; this one is temporary and we have to pay for the right to be here.

Nahuas who have chosen to enter the craft industry as a way of getting ahead use the Spanish word *lucha* to describe what they do to make a living. Catherine Good, who did a study of the craft industry, focusing on the town of Ameyaltepec, named her book *Haciendo la Lucha*, which can be roughly translated as "Struggling to Get Ahead."

Although some craft vendors have permanent stands, most of them sell on the street, or in parks and bus stations. Others work on commission for specific clients. Each artisan has his or her own story. Aron told me:

> In 1970 I would take the bus to Taxco where I used to paint in a hotel and later in a store. One day when I was selling my amates on the street, a man who really liked my work invited me to come and paint for him. He wanted me to decorate lamp shades and plates. I used to earn seventy-eight pesos a week when farmhands in Xalitla earned only three pesos a day. That was good money. Next a man Taxco Viejo became my boss. He had a shop where he made clayware and I went there every day to paint plates.

The way Aron began his career is not typical, because he started off working for fixed wages. Today he no longer goes to Taxco and works for himself at home. I interviewed him in 2006 while he was tracing the outlines for an amate. His wife, wearing glasses, sat at the other end of a large table, applying paint to fill in sections of another amate, while he spoke: "Sometimes people come here to buy my work, but I usually take a bus to Mexico City and to Acapulco to make deliveries to regular clients. If they come to my house I ask 250 pesos for the kind of big painting you see here—the one with an Aztec calendar in the middle."

The business of making and selling crafts has changed over the last fifty years. At first, painting or carving was an extra source of income and artisans grew corn during the wet season, painting or carving during slack periods of the agricultural cycle, or in their spare time. In the case of amate painting, one person would design and draw the picture while other members of the household would do the coloring in. These farmers-artisans would not leave their hometowns to sell what they produced until the dry season, which started as early as January, coming home for major ritual occasions and feasting. Everyone would return to prepare the soil in anticipation of rainfall at the end of May, or in June, to plant, and then weed and transplant chili plants from home gardens to the fields that might be located anywhere from a half hour to two hours away by donkey. Fresh *elotes* (corn on the cob) would be ready in September but the sun-dried corn used to make tortillas was not harvested until later in the fall. Then it was time to start getting ready to hit the road again, usually after making sure that the new crop was stored away.

At first one did not require a lot of money to be an artist. Paint was made from the dyes of local plants, and the clay suitable for making different kinds of clayware could be dug from the ground. Artisans knew what kind of trees had to be cut down to get the right kind of wood for carving masks, bowls, or fish figures. People used the same machetes used in the fields to carve wood. However, it was necessary to go to Iguala to buy brushes, varnish, and, with the introduction of amate painting, a special kind of paper. The paper, made from the bark of trees in a village of Otomis in a neighboring state, was delivered by vendors from that village. The initial cost for starting up would often be covered by other family members, or by close friends who would lend money that could be paid back from the sales upon returning from a trip. An artisan would also need money to pay for boarding a bus in Xalitla after walking there with a load of wares. Heavier but more fragile clayware would be carefully packed in bags made from locally made hemp (*ixtle*) and transported on the back of donkeys. Artisans from towns that were not close to the highway left their donkeys in the care of someone in Xalitla. Initially most artisans could not afford to stay in hotels, but they had to have enough money to pay for food while away from home.

People used to sell handicrafts only in places that could be reached by boarding one of the many buses one could flag down along the side of the highway in Xalitla, to go either to Acapulco or, going the other way, to Cuernavaca. Some bus drivers were reluctant to stop for passengers on the side of the road with bulky packages and big carton boxes full of merchandise. Once they got over their fear about getting lost in downtown Mexico City, vendors started going back and forth to the national capital, which was then booming. It helped to know someone to show you how to navigate the streets on foot as well as how to use the underground subway. Over time the process of making handicrafts became more sophisticated, but also more expensive and complicated. Painters started out by using store-bought water-based paints but soon turned to more expensive acrylics, and wood carvers used commercial sandpaper. With the introduction of electricity in their home villages, artisans started using electric sanders. Carvers had to fabricate smaller objects and go farther afield to get wood as the type of trees needed became depleted, and those specializing in painting wooden objects no longer carved their own. Instead, they bought unpainted animal figures in other towns, like the mestizo town of Palula.

When the Mexican government realized the potential of the craft industry, they set up an agency to provide credit for groups or individuals and warehouses where they would buy directly from artisans. However, many artisan-vendors preferred to slowly build up their own capital or borrow money from relatives who had extra funds. Better-off Nahuas used the money they earned by selling off some of their cattle to buy pickup trucks. They went into the business of becoming wholesalers, buying crafts in neighboring villages from people who could not afford to sell their own crafts. Such Nahua craft merchants provided small advances, usually in kind, to anyone who wanted to carve or paint as a supplementary activity. However, most people who already had some experience as craftsmen and vendors preferred to gradually expand their own businesses to the point where they could buy a vehicle and no longer go by bus. As craft vendors ventured further afield, the cost of transportation also went up. They would look for places with other craft vendors willing to share the cost of lodgings. Some vendors brought their families with them on trips, with children helping out by selling on the street. Such families eventually rented rooms so that they could stay for most of the year in a specific location and continue making their own crafts, sometimes in the same location where they have a stand. Consequently, Nahua children started attending school in places such as Cuernavaca, La Peñita, or San Miguel de Allende. These Nahua artisan-vendors who no longer lived at home most of the time stopped growing corn, but they returned to their hometowns for long vacations, as well as to participate in ceremonies. Most still do so today.

Artisans who do not settle down in one place, but instead continue to make trips to various, sometimes distant, locations, now spend less time producing their own crafts. Instead they buy the crafts of local people who cannot travel themselves, as well as crafts from artisans in other parts of Mexico. But they continue to use their hometowns in the Alto Balsas as their center of operation. However, there is always the risk of getting robbed or being harassed by policemen, although much less so than in the past. Cristobal provides a good example of the career trajectory of a farmer-artisan-vender who eventually became a full-time craft merchant:

> At first people started to struggle to make a better living. A man who is now very old showed us how to make wooden masks. We used to bring tree trunks from San Francisco Zumatlán to make those masks; I was not very good at it but we did it anyways, however we could. We sold the masks in Mexico City in a street with the name of Pensador Mexicano. I would go to Mexico City and come back to start making more masks. After that we changed what we did and went to another place in Mexico City called La Lagunilla. There I found a boss by the name of Rene Flores who bought crafts on commission. He asked if I could also bring him amates and I said yes. I would deliver five or six hundred of them. At that time they were cheap to buy, around fourteen thousand pesos. Nowadays we would say that is expensive but nowadays that would be around five ten pesos a piece (they were selling during a period of high inflation). Afterwards I would leave him wooden figurines: little owls, horses, bulls, and deer.

Like so many craft vendors, Cristobal found a partner, another artisan-vendor, when he was ready to go as far as the Yucatán Peninsula to sell crafts. The fare was not too expensive and they had no trouble selling ten thousand pesos worth of amates on their first trip. They went back home and their second trip was also successful. However, when the crafts business started to decline, it became more challenging to be a traveling vendor. Cristobal and his partner ran into some real challenges during a trip to the resort city of Cancun:

> We had to sleep on the beach, under a plastic sheet. A lady who worked there asked us what had happened so we explained that we did not have enough money to stay in a hotel. She suggested that we go to the island of Cozumel. She told us we would easily be able to sell there. So we boarded a bus and then took a ferry to reach the island. There we sold our amates and returned home.

Like most vendors, Cristobal had to be ready to change both his merchandise and the locations where he sold crafts. As the market for amates dried up, he switched to bracelets and started selling on his own in Mexico City. In order to cover his costs and still have some money left over he had to diversify what he sold, including crafts produced in other regions.

> I also started selling earrings made from stones. I bought those in Queretaro, ready made, with their settings. From that there was a change to another type of necklace that we bought in Tepito. I moved to another street but there were bad thieves there who hit me on my back. Then I moved to Doctor Bertis Street, where I stayed another three years. All they sell there is necklaces, all kinds of them. In 1987 I started going to Tampico with my wife and we still go there from time to time.

Other vendors started to travel further north along the Pacific coast, to Mazatlan, and then to cities close to the American border such as Puerto Peñasco and Tijuana. The income earned by these artisan-vendors enabled families to eat better and also save enough money to build larger houses. As early as 1980, visitors were surprised to see two- or three-story cement houses in places like Ahuehuepan, Ahuelican, and Ameyaltepec. However, not everyone benefited from this craft boom to the same extent. In most towns artisans still market their own products, but this is not the case in San Francisco Zumatlán where most people who carve wooden masks have always sold what they make to middlemen, including Nahua artisan-vendors from other villages. In Maxela most artisans, all women, also sell directly to middlemen.

Today there is a noticeable gap in the standard of living between full-time vendors and artisans who can no longer afford to travel. A handful of wholesalers in places such as Ameyaltepec are considered even by outsiders as "rich Indians." Those wholesalers now own several vehicles as well as second homes in Cancun or Tijuana. They buy some of their crafts from Spanish-speaking artisans. This change in ethnic status was hard to swallow for the inhabitants of Maxela where the Nahuatl language has all but disappeared and where people now considered themselves to be mestizos. In 2010, a woman there who paints for a wholesaler from Ameyaltepec commented: "Those wholesalers have new cars, and they are making money. They come to buy what we paint and then go and sell it. We cannot do that even though we all speak Spanish and they speak Mexicano. They all go to far away places." Today there are half a dozen wholesalers from Ameyaltepec, Ahuehuepan, and San Juan Tetelcingo. Aron, who still makes a living as a full-time amate painter in Xalitla, observed: "To make an amate, especially *historietas* which depict everyday life, takes three days of work. In Ameyaltepec people no longer paint amates because now they are rich merchants. They go to all the ports and some have learned a bit of English to be better salesmen."

Whereas some people who no longer paint have become known for their success in business, at least two Nahua artisans who specialize in painting amates have made a name for themselves in the world of art. These paint-ers, who have been invited to travel abroad to show their work, are seen as real artists, not just craftspeople. They each rent studios, one in the city of Cuernavaca and the other in Chilpancingo, the capital of Guerrero. Own-ers of art galleries took an interest in their work and brought these artists to the attention of art lovers and collectors in Mexico and abroad. When I visited one of them, it cost me five hundred dollars to buy one of his smaller amates, unframed. The limited edition prints that are the specialty of the other artist can be bought online from a dealer in the United States. The income of these artists fluctuates but they have enough to pay for their rent, to feed their families, and to afford the upkeep of the houses they own in the Alto Balsas. Neither owns a car, nor are these artists rich enough to buy city houses.

About thirty amate painters, including several women, have received recognition for their work in local and national competitions organized by the Mexican government, and three of them in turn have also received international recognition. One of them, a man called Aron, whom we met before, told me: "One day some Japanese came to see me. They came with a whole team, including a translator and film crew, first to Chilpancingo, and then here to my house in Xalitla." However, he and other painters also decorate lampshades and bowls to make ends meet. Aron in particular is now finding it hard to make ends meet. When I visited Aron and his wife in 2008, she said: "We are still doing OK but this year sales are very slow. The Mexican economy is not doing well and we no longer see as many tourists. All the vendors we know are complaining that people are no lon-ger buying crafts."

To survive economically, Nahua artisans who are vendors have to also sell crafts originating in other regions, including jewelry made from semi-precious stones imported from Asia. However, increasing competition

among vendors and rising prices for art supplies have made it more difficult to stay in business. The craft boom of the sixties and seventies had
already ended by the eighties. However, people already well established
in the craft business are still able to make a decent living by Mexican standards, even when they no longer grow corn and have to buy most of their
own food. Yet, the majority of small-scale artisan-vendors are slowly being
squeezed out by the craft merchants. Moreover, their children, who did
not have to suffer like their parents or grandparents, find it hard to replicate their parents' success, even if they are willing to work long hours
and have infinite patience. It takes an outgoing personality and cunning to
make a living as a full-time vendor. Evaristo, a former amate painter who
today lives in his hometown, told me about his son's failure to become a
craft vendor:

> My son used to paint and sell. I taught him but he discovered that it was
> no longer worth his while, that he was losing money. Sometimes he would
> spend five thousand pesos for his art supplies and another five thousand for
> transport but he would not earn anything. That is why he decided to cross
> the border and work in Sacramento, in the maintenance of their drainage
> system. He is putting in pipes.

Another man who is now middle aged also emigrated to the United States,
but he is now back in Mexico. He now only paints as a hobby. When I paid
him a visit in 2006 he told me he could no longer make a living as an artist. His main complaint was the low price paid for amates and his inability to sell directly to the clients in Mexico City, the way he did in the past:

> I used to paint a lot and sold my paintings in Mexico City, in the Zona Rosa
> [an exclusive neighborhood] for two thousand pesos at a time the dollar was
> worth seven pesos. But the person who used to buy them from me told me
> to not come any more, that he would come and see me here at my house. He
> and other people started coming here but they only paid me five hundred
> pesos. I could no longer cover my costs and instead I started to take passen-
> gers around in the van I bought when I was in the U.S.

One reason amate paintings lost their value is that several people in the region started mass producing large numbers of them using a system of silk
screens (*sellos*) to print multiple copies of a rough outline that would then

be filled with colors by hand. Professional amate painters are proud that each piece of art is unique and done by hand and they value the quality of their workmanship. In contrast, amates made from silk screen outlines are of low quality. The women in Maxela who are commissioned to fill in the colors do not have much time to finish each piece. They are only paid a few pesos for each one. Low-budget tourists in Mexico do not want to pay much for crafts and in any case cannot tell the difference between an original amate made by hand and one that is mass produced under sweatshop conditions.

Most vendors still carry some amates, including bookmarks made from amate paper, but they have more success selling necklaces and bracelets. However, they have had to become ever more creative in finding new customers and different products. Craft vendors further expanded the range of crafts and other objects for sale and they are always coming up with new ideas. For example, well-known beach resorts have long been a good place for artisans who sell their own work, but there are now too many vendors on the beaches of the Mayan Riviera in Yucatán and the Pacific coast. So people from San Juan Tetelcingo are now teaching foreign tourists staying at beach resorts to paint designs on pottery. And some people who work with stone have learned to make replicas of archeological artifacts that can fool even an anthropologist. However, not everyone can make a go of it. Consequently, many artisan-vendors and their children opt to follow other family members or neighbors who are getting ahead as undocumented workers in the United States.

The artisan who opts to become an undocumented worker as a more viable livelihood strategy represents only one way the world of crafts is connected to the international labor market. Some artisans have been successful, even to the point of being able to expand, precisely because they were able to raise money by first working in the United States. This was the case for Aron:

I went to the U.S. several times but never stayed more than a few months. The first time was in 1981, shortly after I was married. One of my friends had already been in Chicago and he wanted me to go along. He said, "Stop painting and come with me. There they are going to pay you ten dollars an hour." I told him I was not interested, that I would not go even if they would pay me thirty dollars. But he came to my house again and I finally decided to go. I earned twelve dollars an hour working in a factory where they make gas tanks for different models of cars. But I went back home after three months to become a full-time amate painter.

Aron went to the United States as an undocumented migrant worker not only to expand his craft business, but on several occasions he needed extra money for household expenses or emergencies:

The third time was in 1985, the year of the earthquake in Mexico City. That year I went to Los Angeles to work in a plastics factory. I did not like that work at all; once I had to work for twenty-one consecutive days, from six in the afternoon until nine the next morning. That is the year my son was born but there was something wrong with his legs. I immediately returned and we took him to Mexico City for an operation. The bones in his leg healed, but I spent all of my earnings.

Another scenario is one where a former artisan now spends a good part of his life in the United States, yet still does craftwork whenever he comes back to Mexico. I met Bonifacio in the fall of 2012, during one of his return visits. He has been going back and forth between the United States and Mexico for over thirty years, but he started off as a farmer-artisan:

As a young man I used to grow corn. I would sow twenty-five *cuartillos* [pints of seed] and when it rained I would harvest twenty *cargas* [about thirty bushels]. It was to feed my family but I would sometimes sell a part of the harvest. I also cut firewood for sale and shot birds to eat. When the harvest was done, I would carve wooden fish, using a machete. I painted and then sold them in several ports. I also sold masks in the form of a sun, plus I used to sell clay necklaces my wife made.

Bonifacio's experience going back and forth across the border is fairly typical for men his age who are lucky enough to obtain a work visa:

I went to the U.S. for the first time in 1980 to work in onions, apples, and also almonds. I only worked for a short time because I was caught and put in jail [for being undocumented]. I had to sign a piece of paper in which I promised I would not return to the U.S. for another five years. In 1988 I went again, this time to Lincoln [California] were my older brother was living. He had been there since 1979 and was working in landscaping. I arrived at the time of the amnesty of President Reagan and wanted to qualify. When I declared that I had been imprisoned earlier, they told me, "you have paid for what you did." They gave me a renewable, three-month permit. Two years later I got a green card, and then the rose card which allowed me to be a U.S. resident. That will expire in 2014, but I want to renew it.

Bonifacio has returned to Mexico to visit his wife and children many times. Each time he is back he makes extra money by helping other family members to paint designs on wooden fish and gourds that are strung together to make mobiles. He has two full brothers and a dozen half brothers and half sisters, most of whom work and live in the United States. Most of them are undocumented, but he was the only one of them who was an artisan. Of his seven children, all born in Ahuehuepan, the two oldest daughters now work without documents in the United States and the others will eventually follow.

Toribio, another man who routinely goes back and forth to the United States, likewise decorates wooden fish when he is in Mexico. We met his sister Paula in the Introduction. Toribio is an undocumented worker who has until recently had no difficulty getting back and forth across the border. His five children were also born in Ahuehuepan and all but one live with their mother. Toribio plans to stay at home for a while longer because there is not enough work in the United States. During a visit at his house in January 2011 he told me:

> I usually work in the U.S., in Sacramento, for a company that makes equipment for landscaping. Thirty-five people work there, including some *guëros* (whites). However, during the recent recession the owner had to let us go, so there was no more work. It was hard to get more than a day or two of work elsewhere, which made it possible to at least pay for rent and food. But there was not much money left to feed my family in Ahuehuepan. My boss offered to lend me money to tide me over, but I did not want to do that. I thought it would be better to just come home where I could eat tortillas and not have to spend a lot of money. I will go back once there is work again. In the meantime I am painting.

The case of Toribio illustrates that craft work in Mexico still provides an opportunity for people to earn some extra money when they are home.

What he produces is sold by a brother who travels regularly to other parts of Mexico. Another brother, who has never been in the United States, also paints at home in his spare time to supplement his meager income as a rural school teacher.

Although many younger craftspeople have opted for permanent migration to the United States, I have come across cases of return migrants who had no other choice but to work as craft vendors. A case in point is Castulo, who helped his father sell crafts in Mexico City when he was a teenager. Castulo had several older brothers and a sister, all of whom had gone to the United States. He joined them in Los Angeles in 2000, and ten years later he was ready to make his first trip home. He and his common-law wife, whom he had met in the United States, had saved up their money to pay for a wedding in their hometown in Guerrero. She was not aware that she was pregnant with their first child when they left Los Angeles, and her pregnancy prevented them from recrossing the border several months later when returning to their jobs. Their child was born in Mexico, which made it even more difficult for them to go back as a family. The couple decided to attempt another border crossing, leaving the baby in the care of Castulo's sister who had earlier gone back to the village after the death of their mother. After another unsuccessful attempt they decided to move to one of the towns near the Pacific coast to join the vendors from their hometown who were already working there for most of the year. I was in Los Angeles for a visit when I overheard a phone call between Castulo and one of his brothers who had stayed in the United States. Castulo and his wife had just found a better place to sell crafts in the state of Oaxaca.

The craft business is not the only one way to make ends meet. When I asked Toribio how else he managed to make a living now that he was back in Mexico, he said: "I work as an artisan whenever I am at home but I also know how to paint houses and install electrical circuits. With all these jobs together I can pay for my personal expenses and also maintain my family. One does not have to spend much money in my hometown." When I spoke to him in 2012 Toribio planned to go back to the United States to earn the money he needs to put some finishing touches to the house he built with earlier earnings as an undocumented worker. He is confident he will find a way to cross the border once more, even though he "does not have papers." A year later he was still in his hometown after several unsuccessful attempts to cross the border, which is becoming increasingly difficult.

Every town in the Alto Balsas has its own history in terms of when people started working in the United States and how migratory labor is connected to the craft industry. In the case of Maxela, which does not have art vendors, people started to work in the United States much earlier than in other towns. For several decades the men would work in the United States while their wives at home would paint amates for wholesalers. Now that more women are also going to the United States, they still work as artisans whenever they come back for extended visits. In contrast, people from Ameyaltepec did not start migrating to the United States until very recently. In 1940 it was the poorest town in the Alto Balsas, with a very small land base, but the craft industry, especially selling crafts, made it the most prosperous town of the region. There, both men and women are artisans and vendors, and until a few years ago few people needed to go to the United States. But this will change; during my last to trip to Texas, I met several young men who had just arrived from Ameyaltepec.

Carving masks and painting amates are not only a way of making a living but can be a source of personal satisfaction. Nahua painters see themselves as creative artists. However, artisans who go to the United States no longer have an outlet for their creativity. In numerous interviews with current or former migrant workers I have come across only one example where someone was able to apply his artistic talent in the workplace, albeit only for a short while. Fernando, who started painting amates when he was eight years old, became an undocumented worker in 1980. His first job was as a carpenter's assistant, but his employment never lasted more than a few weeks at a time. In 1982, he started working for a small ceramics factory that specialized in garden ornaments and interlocking patio stones:

> One day, during my break, my boss saw me drawing pictures of birds and flowers on a scrap of paper. He liked what he saw and asked me to draw some designs for a new line of patio stones. I drew a figure of a rabbit, then a bird and a tiger, and showed him how I could draw decorative borders. For the next few years I was paid to draw the designs used for molds. As the business expanded, he asked me to recruit more workers from Mexico who did manual labor. But the owner ran into financial difficulties when he was fined for hiring undocumented workers. He was also getting older and the factory was sold to someone who went into a completely different line of products. I lost my job.

Fernando, who still lives and works in the United States, never used his artistic talents again. Instead, he started washing cars that came off the assembly line at a new Ford plant. When I spoke to him in 2007 he was shelving merchandise in a supermarket.

One would think that free trade would have benefited craftspeople in the Alto Balsas, with more export possibilities, lower input costs, and more tourist development. Unfortunately, apart from a few men who became full-time wholesalers, the income of the majority of both artists and craft vendors actually deteriorated after the signing of NAFTA because they were no longer able to supplement their incomes, or at least reduce their cost of living, through part-time farming that had previously been subsidized. They could no longer compete with wholesalers who sell in bulk, or with established artists who have won awards. For the majority of artisans, becoming undocumented workers became the only way they could get ahead. However, for those who do not succeed in crossing the border, or for craftspeople who are sent back to Mexico, the Mexican arts and craft industry still represents a better option than working as an unskilled laborer or trying to eke out a living from the land.

3

"No One Lives There"

Adrian is standing in front of the house he built with money earned in Los Angeles. It is a beautiful July day, and not too hot, because it is still the rainy season. The hills in the background are green, with lush vegetation, unlike the barren desert-like look of the land six months ago. He will be staying until the end of the year because it is his turn to serve as vice-mayor of his town. Adrian is thinking out loud:

> Why did I spend so much on a big house? It is much bigger than what I need, and we have only used it twice. I could have spent my money on other things. My children will not live here when they are grown up. They hardly even know this town. My youngest son does not have a clue what I'm talking about when I mention the names of the places where I used to grow corn or leave my father's animals.

I met Adrian the day before at a party to celebrate the *quinceañera*, or coming of age, at the fifteenth birthday of the daughter of one of his compadres (the father of his godchild). After drinking at his compadre's house all the guests walked back to his house where his wife was preparing a meal. We entered though the gate of a walled-in compound consisting of a patio surrounded by three spacious rooms made of poured cement. During my next two stays, two years later, then again in the winter of 2011, I noticed that the doors and windows of his house were shut tight and bolted.

It does not cost as much to build and maintain a house in rural Mexico as it does in the United States. In the Alto Balsas urban lots are free since its inhabitants are entitled to such lots as citizens of indigenous communities, where the land where one has the right to build a house is still held in common. The main costs are buying construction materials and paying for a bricklayer and his assistants. Digging away part of a hillside or building a retaining wall with stones would add to the costs. When Guadencio and his wife Angelina had saved up enough money after working for six years in the United States they built a house that was not too extravagant. That was in 2006. They had to send fourteen thousand dollars to Mexico, although she thought the house they had built should have cost less. I saw that house when I was in Mexico. By comparison a new bungalow in the outskirts of the American city where they were then living would have cost them at least two hundred thousand dollars. I saw another, bigger house still under construction in one town in the Alto Balsas in 2010. I did not ask the owner, who had just come back from Houston to overlook its construction, what it would cost him in total; but in pointing out what still needed to be done he mentioned the cost of a brand-new metal door (two thousand pesos or less than two hundred dollars) and four metal windows, with shutters and their handles (four thousand pesos or less than four hundred dollars). In 2006, I hired a bricklayer to build a self-standing ecological composing toilet for me in the town in the Alto Balsas where I was then living. It was made out of Mexican bricks, had a roof, and the inside walls were plastered. It cost me less than a thousand dollars. During my last trip to Guerrero in 2013 I was told that the cost of cement had gone up considerably and that it would now cost more for construction materials, but the wages of the people who mix the cement and do the digging are still less than two hundred pesos (twenty dollars) a day.

Migrant workers used to think that they would eventually live in such houses when they retired, or use it as a fallback if a serious illness forced them to return home. But these same workers realize that their children, once they are grown up, will no longer want to live in a village where there are no jobs. If you go back there by yourself, to finally spend some time in that house built years ago, you will not be able to enjoy your grandchildren. Yet undocumented migrant workers continue to build new houses in Mexico. Relatives back home cannot understand why they would not do so. In 2006 Magdalena told me: "My nephew Marcos has been in the U.S. for eleven years and he has not come back once. He does not want to build a house, but what will he do if he and his family have to come back to Mexico? If you have a house, you have somewhere to live, something you can fall back on." It so happens that I spoke to Marcos in Sacramento in the fall of 2012, where he told me he might build a house in Mexico after all, but for reasons other than those provided by his aunt Magdalena:

> So far I have not built a house in Mexico because it does not make much sense; it would just stay empty and the corners would gradually crumble away. But the other day I was talking to my wife; I told her it might be a good idea to build a house after all, because her father, who is a vendor in San Blas, would have to work for a long time before he had enough money to have a good house built in his hometown. He would be able to use the new house.

Although some migrants born in Mexico might still end up building a house, as in the case of Marcos, I have not come across any U.S.-born children of migrants who are thinking about building a house in the place where their parents were born.

The types of houses seen in Mexico, the changes in house construction over time, and how those houses are used can tell us a lot about both migrants and those left behind. In the last chapter we saw how the construction of better houses started during the craft boom. Even before that, going back to the thirties, some families were already better-off. Although older people may emphasize how poor they used to be, there were noticeable wealth differences, and even exploitation, in the Alto Balsas. Inequalities were reflected in the kind of houses owned. Prior to 1940, better-off families lived in larger houses with thatched roofs, double crossbeams, and well-made wooden doors and windows. In contrast, everyone else had less durable roofs made of palm and window openings without frames. People with somewhat greater resources started using corrugated tarpaper or tin sheets (*laminas*). After 1940 the more prominent families switched to adobe houses with tile roofs. A house with plaster and whitewashed adobe brick walls, an inner courtyard and a tile floor, was a sign of prestige.

Most towns in the Alto Balsas had three or four families who not only owned bigger houses but as many as a dozen *yuntas* (pairs of oxen and yokes) to plow the land. Those families who could afford to hire a young woman to help grind the corn that was consumed daily were considered to be rich. Prosperous Nahua farmers and cattlemen not only employed men to handle the large wooden plows to break the soil but rented out *yuntas*, charging eight *cargas* of maize (four *cargas* per ox) from the harvest. These men rented out to poorer neighbors as well as to farmers from other towns. Most people in the Alto Balsas region had access to what is designated as communal land, but some families owned a lot more arable land than others. Other people did not have their own oxen and plows even if they owned their own land. The farmhands who worked for those rich neighbors were paid in corn. Those same farmhands cultivated some maize of their own on steep hillsides, using only hand tools. They resented the fact that they had to contribute their labor for free to repair communal fences to protect cornfields from the pastures used only by those who owned cattle. Such differences in both wealth and access to the tools needed for one's livelihood, as well as whether or not one had gone to school, went hand-in-hand with status distinctions that influenced who one was allowed to marry. I have met undocumented workers in the United States who still have painful memories of such class discrimination. Aureliano recalled:

> I am now separated; things just did not work out in part because of ongoing frictions with my mother-in-law. When I was a young man I became friends with her father but he told me that his wife would never allow me to marry their daughter. I was a nobody, because we were very poor. My father, who was born in another town, had no land and I worked as a day laborer. I never went to school [at this point in the interview, he broke into tears]. Eventually we did get married in Mexico but only after I had gone to the United States for a couple of years. I came back wearing good clothes and enough money so I could build a house. Only then did her parents give their daughter permission to marry me.

Aureliano's story illustrates how migration to the United States not only enabled this young man to get married but to obtain at least some respect he did not have before.

The movement of migratory workers to the United States plus the craft boom changed the existing status quo in communities in the Alto Balsas as wealth differences became less pronounced. More families started to build houses with adobe-brick walls and clay-roof tiles. In the early fifties houses with flat roofs made out of poured concrete, and walls made from cement blocks and bricks, started appearing. Although not as cool on hot days as thatch-roofed houses and mud walls, houses made from cement and mortar kept out scorpions and were less likely to catch on fire. Flat roof houses with two stories became a new sign of wealth and social status. Nowadays having painted exterior walls or a parabolic antenna is the distinguishing feature of families deemed to be rich. But these are not necessarily the same families as those who dominated the village economy in 1940. Even once very poor families live in cement houses. One person expressed this change in the status quo in the following manner: "There used to be rich people here but none are alive anymore. All of their families have gone downhill. Now there are lots of artisans as well as people who work in the U.S. Today's poor are those who still live in the adobe and tile houses once built by their grandparents." Several people explained this reversal in social status by the fact that the children of those who were rich in the past squandered their inheritance.

The way individual and family fortunes in the region have changed over time, and the relationship between the type of housing and income is actually more complicated. In one town a man who owned cattle and lent money at exorbitant rates never built an adobe house. He was a miser who never went to restaurants when he visited Iguala. However, he did buy a truck and became a wholesaler. Sometimes the children of parents who were prosperous also went to the United States, such as Maura, now working as a cleaner in Sacramento. In addition, some poor people who worked hard did much better than others.

Francisco, today the owner of a van, used to live in a small house with a roof made of *carton* (corrugated tarpaper). His father had to rent oxen to plow his land. Francisco was an extremely hard worker who grew more than enough corn so that he was able to sell more than half of his harvest. After preparing his land and sowing his crops he would buy crafts to sell in Nayarit, Cancun, and Merida. After each harvest he would again sell his corn to enable him to buy more merchandise, including unpainted masks and clayware from artisans in other villages. His children helped out with the painting so that their father would not have to buy more expensive finished clayware and masks for resale. Francisco went directly from living in a mud hut, where some of his children were born, to building a house with a cement roof. Of his six children, two sons and one daughter also became craft vendors. One son drives the family van back and forth to Iguala transporting paying passengers and sometimes takes people to Cuernavaca, the first leg in their journey to the U.S. border. All of these children either live in their father's house or use it whenever they stay in their home village. None have gone to the United States.

Whether working in the craft industry or as undocumented migrant workers, young people generally live with their parents for a couple of years during the times they are back home, even after they get married. Those who work in the United States send money to their parents who oversee the building of a cement house. I know of several cases where a single woman helped her parents build their first good house or remodel an older cement house that still had a dirt floor. Single men anticipate they will eventually bring a wife to a new house being built with the money they send. If a son is already living with a woman they will not have an elaborate wedding until the house is ready. Such houses, built in stages, could take anywhere from three to twenty years to complete. In the past, most people were able to erect a new house on the same urban lot occupied by their parents. Nahuas generally follow the rule that a couple must live close to the man's father; several married brothers may live in adjacent houses, or simply build additional rooms. When there is no more room to expand it becomes necessary to ask for a new plot of land, usually at the edge of town. Once the site is chosen, one has to start buying building material: bags of cement, gravel, sand, wooden poles, bricks, and metal rods. Nowadays these can be delivered by dump trucks. I have visited many houses with a pile of large bricks, *tabiques*, occupying a section of someone's yard. If the money runs out, the actual construction work cannot begin. Some men who were trained as bricklayers or masons can do a lot of the work themselves, but in most cases people hire a mason who in turn finds hired hands.

Forty years ago everyone in each town always pitched in whenever someone living in that town started building a house, but nowadays communal unpaid labor is used only for the finishing touches. I have witnessed and taken part in such work parties. Young men, usually paid help from another village, mix the cement and gravel by hand, to be shoveled into square metal buckets. Others carry containers of wet cement, perched on their shoulders, up a wooden ladder to reach the top of one of the cement walls that has already been finished. Metal rods sticking up from these walls may be used for a second story to be added later, and a provisional ceiling made out of rough wooden planks is in place. Someone starts pouring out the cement to be spread out under the watchful eyes of the master mason. This is where neighbors help out for free. On one occasion I also participated by inserting crumpled up pieces of paper into the cracks between the wooden planks; that way not too much cement will drip through onto the floor below. In the meantime women prepare food for a celebratory meal.

The logistics of getting a house built when a person is still living and working in the United States can get complicated. He or she usually relies on a trusted family member in Mexico to make all the arrangements. It is easier to give instructions and receive reports if the contact person in Mexico has a phone with a landline. But most people in Mexican village have to walk to someone else's house or to a store to take incoming phone calls, which are announced through a loudspeaker. In some towns without phone lines, people have to travel to another town and wait for a call at a prearranged time. It is sometimes easier for a person to travel to Mexico and personally supervise the work. However, most couples in the United States come back to Mexico only when all the work has been completed. It is customary for them to save up enough money so that they can combine their return trip to take possession of a new house with a big wedding. I have witnessed several such weddings in Mexico, where bride and groom already have children who act as bridesmaids. Rarely does the new family stay in Mexico for more than a couple of months, not to be seen again until many years later. Big weddings and having a house built are both expensive, so some couples try to economize. Moreover, there could be friction about financial matters if the people in the United States and those in Mexico have difficulties getting along. Angelina told me:

> We had a small house built in Ahuehuepan, a house with only one story, but it does have a door, windows, and an inside toilet. At first I wanted a bigger house but I changed my mind. Initially I though we would only go to the U.S. to earn money and then return. I wanted to start a small business in Mexico. But things did not turn out that way. Another reason I did not

want to return has to do with my mother-in-law, with whom I had a falling out; she cheated me when I was escorting her back to Mexico. She did the same when we later sent her money for building our house. I think that my mother-in-law spent too much money and it was not all for the house.

Angelina and her husband had originally met in the United States and their children were born in Houston. Like so many undocumented workers, they took a trip back to their hometown when their house was ready, and stayed for several months so that their two sons could get to know their paternal grandparents. However, their house did not stay locked up for long after they went back to the United States. Angelina's now widowed mother-in-law is currently living there with two of her younger children.

Owning one's own house in Mexico does not necessarily mean that a couple will end up staying in that house, not even during return visits. Bulfrano's story illustrates the reasons why this might happen:

> I went back to Mexico to make all the arrangements for my house to be built in 1997. It is located on the side of a hill, close to the cemetery. Our house was finished in 1999 but at that time it still did not have a cement floor. That is why we all stayed with my parents on two other occasions when we visited our hometown. The cement floor was poured in 2008 and only then did we store the *trastes* (dishes and furniture) we were given during our wedding. Before that my parents kept all of our belongings in their house. But up to now we still have not stayed in that house. It is still not connected to the electrical grid and we do not have running water.

During a visit to Mexico in the fall of 2011 I had another look at the house of Adrian (the man mentioned in the beginning of this chapter). I did so while taking photos of other houses that were not being used. I had already found someone willing to be my guide, and I had set aside a day for each of several barrios. The first day he took me to see houses in his own barrio, including one located at the end of town on a piece of land where people used to grow corn. In walking along a footpath he would sometimes point out a house in the distance, at other times we walked right up to it to get a good look. Each time I was told who owned the house and where they had gone. My guide insisted that none of the houses were abandoned because they all had owners who could return. When I asked about who is in charge of looking after those houses, I learned that a relative usually comes by once in a while to sweep up the areas outside of the house, although in only one case did someone with a key actually enter to check inside. It turns out that many of those houses are used to store the household items normally given to the married couple at their wedding. On the first day we covered twenty houses. Two days later we did over half of a larger barrio until we ran out of time. I did not take any more photos, nor was my guide able to take off yet another day to visit the remaining barrios. Instead I sat down with Magdalena and a neighbor who helped me to create a list of all of the remaining families whose houses had been locked for at least the last couple of months. When added up, it turned out that there were 105 houses where no one lived, not including additional houses not yet ready for habitation. That number represents more than a third of all of the houses in that town.

A year later, during my first trip to Atlanta, I stayed with Magdalena's nephew Juan and his wife, whom I had met in Mexico six years earlier. I still remember how surprised I had been to overhear their two children speaking English, and to see them eating a bowl of corn flakes instead of homemade tortillas at the house of their uncle in Guerrero during that earlier visit in Mexico. Juan and Jessica now have seven children, only one of whom was born in Mexico. During my first visit to their home in Atlanta in 2011, I showed the family all of the photos of locked-up houses I had taken the previous fall in their hometown. One of the children turned to his father and asked, "Does Grandpa live in a ghost town?"

4

"I Feel Sorry for Them"

One of the consequences of migratory labor is the absence of a father. The separation of couples puts a strain on marriages; sometimes a man in the United States finds another partner and forgets about his wife and children in Mexico. At other times a woman who is herself a migrant gives up on a husband who has been deported for repeated offenses for drunk driving, and she stays in the United States. Yet in most cases children stay with their mother until they are ready to strike out on their own. I did not anticipate the possibility that children might not have any contact with either parent for a long time. I first became aware of such scenarios when I was visiting a family in Mexico. We were all sitting in a small clearing in front of their house, built on the side of a hill, when I saw four small hands reaching out from behind a stone wall that separates the clearing from the street below. The eyes of two children peered out over the top. First their heads and later the rest of their bodies came into view. They had climbed up the wall by stepping on the stones jutting out from the masonry. My host, the woman with whom I was talking, told me that she was their aunt and that they had come for a visit. She commented that their mother was currently living in Houston, and that the children's father had gone to the United States long before their mother's departure. She knew that they were being raised by their grandmother, who still had children of her own, but she still felt sorry for them. I later discovered that in the town where I conducted my survey, at least six sets of children had not seen their parents for over ten years.

Ricardo's mother left without him at a time when she was still breast-feeding her son. Two older brothers were at that time attending elementary school. By the time I met these students they were well into their teens; they had still not seen their parents. Their paternal grandparents who were taking care of them did not want the boys to continue their studies in the village high school. Instead, they wanted their grandchildren to help out at home and in the fields. One of their neighbors told me that her daughter was not going to leave her children like that. Her disapproval indicates that for a mother to leave her children behind for a long time, even if left in the care of aging grandparents, goes against local norms. However, despite social reproach, couples sometimes leave children behind for various reasons, including the dangers of border crossings. Ricardo's parents, both working in a garment factory in downtown Los Angeles, a city known for its high crime rate and gangs, did not want their children exposed to bad influences.

Isabel left her four children ages eight, six, three, and two in the care of her parents when she crossed the border to join her husband. One of her neighbors later told me: "The youngest child cried a lot when his mother left him, and he kept crying for a long time. For the next few years, whenever he saw a plane pass overhead in the sky, he would call out 'maa . . . maa . . . maa.'" One couple migrated together, leaving behind Graciela, then only two months old. When she was sixteen Graciela did not eat for three days while trying to cross the border to find her parents; she was apprehended and held in custody for a month before being deported. In the end she did see her father, but in Mexico, in the city of Iguala; that was in 2011, soon after he too had been deported. The long absence of both parents is hard on grandparents who are getting frail and elderly. At first they do not mind preparing more food and enjoy the company of young children. However, as the children grow up and become teenagers, they can no longer cope.

Initially I thought that children growing up in Mexico without parents would have little in common with children their own age in the United

States. I did not think such children were likely to meet, especially if they were not related. But life is full of surprises, as I found out when spending a week with a family in Los Angeles. They had three children, whose bedroom was vacated to accommodate the visiting anthropologist. I was sitting in their living room as those children watched a movie about a boy in Mexico who had crossed the border to find his mother whom he had not seen for four years. Little did I know, when I remarked that I knew children in their hometown who were like the boy portrayed in the movie, that the fourteen-year-old daughter of this family had met one of the children in Mexico to whom I was referring. Her mother explained:

> We all went back to Mexico in 2006 for our wedding and stayed in our hometown for eight months. Our two oldest children had already started school here in Los Angeles, so we enrolled them in the village school where my oldest daughter learned how to read and write Spanish. While attending that school she met and became good friends with a young woman who had not seen her parents for several years. She told my daughter she hoped we would never leave her as in the case of her own parents. Last August, my daughter, who now has a passport, flew to Mexico on her own for a short visit, but she did not see that young woman again because her friend was then living in another part of Mexico helping an uncle who is a vendor.

The family with whom I stayed in Los Angeles represents a new trend of couples who raise their children in the United States. Up until about fifteen years ago, the majority of women stayed in Mexico while their husbands made trips back home. During the bracero era their wives and children knew exactly when they would return. But when migrants started to cross the border without documents, their return became less predictable. Nevertheless, it was so easy to cross the border that children continued to have contact with their fathers. As border crossing became more difficult, with longer periods between home visits, children and married women suffered from emotional strain. Wives had to take on more responsibilities. A family doctor who worked for two years in one of the Nahua towns provided me with insights into the psychological stress suffered by women who do not see their husbands for several years at a time, and sometimes even longer:

> There are a lot of cases of depression here; most of my patients are women whose husbands have been away for a long time. Those women keep

hoping that their husbands will come back and they spend a lot of time in the church early in the morning singing and praying. They tell me how they feel like they have been abandoned. Those women want someone to listen to them.

Some men continue to send remittances to their wives in Mexico even if they have no intention of going back, and have a mistress or a new partner in the United States. Nevertheless, they will take in an older child once he or she is ready to start their own life as an undocumented worker. However, many women complain that their husband is not sending enough money for the support of their children. The plight of women who have been completely abandoned by their husbands is particularly sad. When I first arranged to rent a room in Mexico from a family, the woman in charge was the wife of a man then living in California. At that time she was living with her husband's elderly parents and Josefa, her sister-in-law who had five children. When I stayed with them for three months the following year, my landlady and her two children had just gone to California. Now Josefa, who had been abandoned several years earlier, was the only person left in charge of looking after the older couple. Neither her ex-husband nor her in-laws send sufficient money to defray the cost of running the household:

> My husband left us eight years ago when he took off with another woman. At first he would talk to me once in a while but I have not heard from him for five years. He doesn't really support us; once in a while he might send us some money, only twenty or thirty dollars. My in-laws have their own families to support and cannot afford to send us much money so I grow my own corn.

Josefa had to be resourceful. One day, when the electrical circuit in my room shorted out, Josefa changed into blue jeans and returned with a pair of pliers and wire to repair a burned-out socket. Several years later, when her mother-in-law in Mexico got sick and her father-in-law was bedridden, she was nursing two people as well as raising her own children.

Women and children are not the only ones who suffer emotionally or have conflicting feelings; men who come back to Mexico on their own miss their families living in the United States yet they do not like leaving their elderly parents once they leave again. I met Victor when he was on his way to collect firewood for his mother, who is now living by herself. He told me:

> I have been here since December. I have five children in the U.S. and just spoke over the phone to my daughter who has never seen my village. I told her how beautiful it is here. Right now I find it hard to leave; I like it here and my mother needs me. I also have two grandmothers; one cries a lot when I tell her I want to go back to be with my wife and children.

Another story illustrated the emotional stress felt by men. Basilio was away for a long time, although he used to come home for short visits. His wife, who never went to the United States, did a lot of traveling in Mexico as a vendor. Their children would accompany her on business trips until most of them also left to join their father. On one of his visits to Mexico, Basilio discovered that his wife had suddenly died. He was very upset and regretted not having spent more time at home. He cried openly. When I met him in the United States in the fall of 2011, this man, who can no longer work due to his age and his health, was living in his daughter and son-in-law's apartment; he now spends most days babysitting his grandson whose parents work during the day.

Basilio represents the generation of migrant workers whose wives stayed in Mexico. Between 1970 and 1990, these men usually came back for visits every couple of months. When absent, they sent back enough money to cover the cost of food and clothing for their dependents, plus the money needed to remodel a house or build a new one. In the town where I did my survey, I was told that men without documents were just as likely to support their families in Mexico and to spend time with them as those who were legalized as a result of the 1986 amnesty. It is hard to generalize about this period for the entire Alto Balsas; I calculate that in the town where I did my survey, families where the main breadwinner was an international migrant constituted less than a quarter of approximately three hundred households in 1990. Only seven migrants, all men, had work permits. In contrast, in a neighboring town, where men started migrating to the United States about fifteen years earlier, more than half of the migrants were documented in 1990. By the middle of the first decade of this century, when I got to know both of these towns fairly well, the situation was very different. Over two-thirds of a now much larger number of households in both towns either had adult members in the United States or the families did not live in Mexico at all. Most are undocumented. I noticed that people who "have papers" still go back and forth fairly regularly, while most of those who are undocumented have not been home for a long time.

I know which people are documented because I had met most of them by the end of my tenth trip, in 2006. In the town where I did my survey there are now eight workers "with papers." I did interviews with four of these legal migrant workers and have interacted with some of their children in both Mexico and the United States. These documented workers come home on a regular basis, even if the entire family in now living in the United States. For example, Rogelio, whose wife is not documented, has come back to stay at his parents' house in Mexico twice between the beginning of 2012 and the end of January 2013. The first time he came to attend the funeral of his father's brother, to whom he was very close, and the second time when his father was sick, to help bring him back and forth to the hospital in Iguala and to make sure that he was taking his medications properly once he was living at home again. I first met Bonifacio, a documented worker whose wife and younger children have never been in the United States, in the fall of 2004 when I attended the graduation of his five-year-old son from kindergarten in Mexico. Bonifacio has been back many times to deal with family emergencies, to spend time with his wife and children during the big festivals held twice a year, and to attend major school events, usually held in June. His brother, whose wife and children live in the United States, also makes regular return visits; in 2009 this brother stayed for eight months in Mexico to attend to his elderly mother, who was ill. In stark contrast, only two of approximately twenty-five undocumented men whose wives stay at home in Mexico now make frequent home visits. Most undocumented couples whose children were born in the United States have never returned, although some of their American-born children make brief visits once they are old enough to apply for a passport. But their parents might never again see their parents, grandparents, or uncles and aunts in Mexico.

The degree to which men are involved in the upbringing of their children, the quality of relationships among couples, and the extent to which men or women are involved in the care of elderly parents vary considerably, as is the case in all societies. However, being undocumented puts severe constraints on the ability of many parents to spend time with their children or fulfill their obligations to other family members. I consider a dysfunctional American immigration policy to be largely responsible for the emotional trauma, tragedies, and family separations described in this chapter. American authorities do not allow millions of workers who are essential to the U.S. economy to work legally. They are also making it almost impossible for those migrant Mexican workers to cross the border. The women in the United States who leave their children in the care of someone in Mexico would probably not have made this painful decision if they and their husbands had been able to go more easily back and forth across the border. Children and teenagers would have more contact with their fathers and with their siblings. All the people with whom I have spoken wish they had the opportunity to apply for a work permit in the United States and at the same time spend more time with their loved ones in Mexico.

Migrants started coming home for visits less frequently when it became more challenging to cross the border. Around that time young single women were developing relationships with men from their hometown whom they met in the United States. Such couples invariably went back to their hometown for their wedding, but neither they nor their American-born children would visit their hometowns very often and certainly not as family units. Starting around the mid-nineties, many more young couples already living together, or recently married in Mexico, started migrating together, hence few young people were left in most towns. Martha, at age seventeen, was the only one still living with her parents; all her brothers and sisters were in the United States. Everything had gone well as long as their children could still help out at home, and before Martha's mother started to have problems with her legs. It became more difficult to run the household with only two children left with their aging parents. I used to visit their house when this couple's youngest son was still helping out in the fields. I noticed that he used to boss his younger sister around and poke fun at her. I also saw that Martha's parents were always asking her to do something for them, even when Martha was doing her homework: "Come quickly! Start preparing the dough for the tortillas. Quick! Turn off the hose; the tank is overflowing. A neighbor's pig has entered the yard. Chase it away! Your father is back from the fields. Help take off the saddle. Martha! Martha! Martha!" When Martha's brother left home to join one of his older brothers in the United States in 2010, he could no longer tease his sister, but Martha now had more chores to do. She had just graduated from the town's high school so she could now stay at home to help out more. Neither of her parents had gone to school, so they depended on Martha to write messages or read any notices delivered to their door.

Martha's father was strict with his daughter and would not give her permission to meet boys. Her only outlet was playing for a small orchestra in church functions. Then she started receiving handwritten love notes from a young man who had just come back from working in the United States. Daniel, who is older than Martha, had worked in the United States for a couple of years and was ready to look for a wife. I had known about their secret courtship since 2008, but Martha's favorite aunt told me her father was not to know. When Daniel's announced his interest in marriage three years later, Martha announced that she was not yet ready. She told her parents that she wanted to stay home and help them for a while longer, that she was not yet ready to take on the responsibility of running her own household, or working for a mother-in-law. Yet before the end of 2012, the young couple eloped. Martha moved in with Daniel and her new mother-in-law, whose husband had died several years earlier. The three of them started living together in a house that Daniel had arranged to be built while working in the United States. The new couple was hoping to make a new life for themselves north of the border. Two days after the elopement, a teacher in a neighboring town performed a civil marriage on the patio at his house. Both sets of parents were present at that ceremony and signed the necessary papers. One of the witnesses told me:

> Here it is legal for girls as young as thirteen to have a civil marriage. State officials are happy to receive their payment and they don't care if the couple is not mature enough. The parents are in favor because they think that if a boy only makes a promise to marry a girl, and then goes off to the U.S., he might find another girl on the other side of the border. If they get married in Mexico, they will have a more secure relationship.

In Mexico, a civil marriage is separate from a religious one, and the Catholic Church does not recognize civil marriages, nor do they allow couples to be married until they are at least eighteen years old. The local priest would not give his blessing when one of Martha's brothers, Efrain, wanted to marry his girlfriend. He was then only seventeen and she was fourteen. Instead, they too had a civil marriage before they left to go to the

United States where they started living with another one of Martha's older brothers in Sacramento, California. Having a civil marriage can become useful in the United States especially if the girl is still underage, as in the case of Bulfrano Juarez and his wife Ofelia:

> I got married when I was seventeen years old and Ofelia was only fourteen. Yes, we were just kids. We had a civil marriage in Mexico before going to San Marcos, California. Ofelia got pregnant so we went to a hospital so she could deliver her first baby. There a social worker reported a rape case because she was underage. Luckily we had our Mexican marriage certificate and I was not prosecuted.

Today, young people do not want to follow the example of the previous generation, when many children never really got to know their father, and, in some cases, their mother. They do not want to start families where children get separated, or where some children are Americans while others are illegal aliens. Unfortunately, there is no guarantee that a recently married couple will make it across the border, even if they already have a job waiting for them; a man may succeed in crossing the border, while his wife does not. Even if a young couple reaches a final destination, they still have many hurdles to overcome. Martha's brother Efrain and his young bride reached Sacramento, but life was not easy. Efrain had a hard time getting a job because he looked so young; his own relatives thought that he was not strong and mature enough to have a full-time job. Yet he is now working eight hours a day making sandwiches so he can support a baby, with a second one on the way. I had known Efrain in Mexico, so I wanted to say hello when I was in the same neighborhood where he was working. I discovered that he is no longer the happy kid I remember. Unlike his wife, who had arrived in the United States when she was only four years old, Efrain is not eligible to become legalized under a procedure for the offspring of undocumented workers set up under President Obama. Efrain and all of the other people mentioned in this chapter illustrate the human costs associated with having an integrated economy that does not allow an internationalized labor force to easily move back and forth between the country where they are working and the country they still call home.

5

"It Used to Be Easy to Cross the Border"

Prior to the mid-80s, it was easy for undocumented workers to cross the border, although it sometimes took several attempts. Some people had no difficulty at all. Sergio, who first went to the United States in the early eighties, told me: "The first time I crossed the border I paid three hundred dollars to a *coyote* [someone paid to smuggle people across the border] in Mexicali. It was easy because there was only one barrier and you could jump across. In 1987 I crossed at Tijuana and paid four hundred dollars." In the early nineties migrants would sometimes succeed in entering the United States at regular border crossings without proper documentation by simply making a verbal declaration that they were born in San Diego or El Paso. They would refer to this method of crossing the border as going "*por la linea*" (through the lineup). Today the situation is quite different, as noted by Bulfrano in 2012: "Before it used to be easy to cross the border; each time I used a different coyote and we were never caught. I would always cross by going through the hills, sometimes through Tecate and once through San Luis de Rio Colorado. But nowadays it is hard to cross and the coyotes charge four and even five thousand dollars." I witnessed how easy it was to bypass U.S. border patrols in 1981 when I inadvertently smuggled across two young men. I was driving back from Mexico to the university in Canada where I was then teaching. Going through the Mexican state of Sonora, at the end of my first stretch of what would be three days of driving, I picked up two hitchhikers before reaching the border. They told me they were Mexicans who lived on the American side and routinely went back and forth. I showed my passport to border officials but was surprised that the two men were not once asked to show *any* identification. Several miles north of the border I encountered another checkpoint and again proceeded without a problem. I wondered whether the man who looked at my passport thought I was a farmer traveling with hired hands. A few miles further on the men confessed that they were really *mojados* ("wetbacks"), one of whom had earlier spent some time in Texas as an undocumented worker. They told me, "*maestro* [teacher], we did not want to tell you the truth before because you might have become nervous when we were crossing those border checks." This scenario would not happen today.

After the 1986 amnesty some Mexicans living in the United States were given work permits that allowed them to go back and forth across the border. It now became possible for the undocumented relatives of those who were legalized to cross the border without having to pay a coyote. One man told me: "My uncle had his papers, so he would just drive across the border and pick me up in Tijuana. When we drove back across the border I would pretend to be his son. We have the same last name." Several men from one town who have U.S. work permits and residency status facilitate the transportation of household belongings and other goods. Magdalena explained how this works:

> I know Pancho, a bachelor who went to Los Angeles. He has his papers and owns a truck. People without papers meet him in Tijuana. They give him their belongings, as well as things for undocumented workers living in California. He mainly transports packages; each package has the name of its owner and of the person to whom it is going. The person who receives a package pays him twenty or thirty dollars.

It is easier to bring objects across the border than people, and not everyone makes it across. Coyotes escorting people on foot might run away when they see the Border Patrol coming and sometimes less experienced coyotes get lost. By the mid-nineties it had already become more difficult to enter the United States, and the costs started to creep up. More migrants were turned back, but the majority still eventually ended up crossing the border after several tries. Bulfrano, whom we will meet later in connection with the textile industry, recounted:

> When I first came to Los Angeles in 1994 I paid 350 dollars to a coyote, and when I went to Mexico for my wedding in 1997 it cost 450 dollars on the way back. In 2003 I went back to Mexico by myself to surprise my father on his birthday and it cost me $1,700. I paid the same amount a year later. In 2008 the whole family went back to stay for eight months and we paid $2,800. We have not been back since.

As it became more difficult to cross the border, undocumented migrants had to be more creative in finding ways to enter the United States. Baltazar recalls how he used to cross the border to go back and forth to visit his family:

> The way I used to make my way back to Los Angeles was as follows; once I knew how to get to the border all I had to do was to climb over a fence near San Isidro; that was more like a fence used for chicken coops. I went alone, without a coyote, but someone then had to come and pick me up by car and cross a border patrol located further along the highway. The driver, who knew exactly which lane to use, would have to find someone else to go behind him to look carefully when they changed Border Patrol officers [for about three minutes before a new shift, no one was minding that checkpoint].

People who succeed in crossing often have a long journey ahead of them before they reach their final destination. According to Genaro: "My brother-in-law, who had been in the U.S. before, took me across the border. Twice we were picked up and sent back to Mexico, but on the third try we made it across. We crossed the border at Matamoros/Brownsville, like all those who leave my hometown. But we still had to walk two days, all the way to Houston [they had several rides for that portion of the trip]."

As it became even more difficult to cross the border, undocumented workers had to take more risks and take less accessible routes, including walking across the desert in Arizona. Some were still able to cross the hills near Tijuana but had to walk further. Jessica found her first trip through mountainous terrain difficult: "We were walking through the hills at night, everyone holding on to a long rope. I could not see where I was going. We all carried sticks so we could feel where we were stepping, and sometimes the person walking behind would hit the person in front by mistake." Her crossing did not go without a hitch; Jessica stumbled across a muddy patch of ground, and lost one of her tennis shoes. Her sister-in-law, Angelina, faced other challenges when she crossed the border for the first time after their wedding in Mexico. Her husband, Rogelio, is one of the lucky ones who has a work permit, so he had no trouble driving back to California. But Angelina and three other women had to take a bus to Tijuana. A week later she had still not been able to find a reliable coyote. Food and hotels were expensive; she ran out of money and couldn't even make a phone call. Angelina, who finally made it across the border, has so far not returned to Mexico. In contrast, another couple has been back and forth several times.

Jessica and Juan, the couple in Sacramento, usually travel together on the way back to the United States. However, their five children go separately. All but the oldest son were born in the United States, so four went by airplane to Tijuana once they knew their parents have arrived safely. There they were met by their uncle Rogelio who is documented and owns a truck. He would clear customs and immigration with the children and then drive them to their home in California. The oldest son, now eighteen, went back and forth on his own several times, assuming the identity of a cousin. He is fluent in English, so he easily passes for an American and would tell the border officials that he was making a short trip to Mexico to visit one of his relatives.

Delfino, whom we have met several times, told me about his first two trips back to the United States when he was a teenager:

> The first time I walked though the hills at night, together with a lot of other people from Ahuelican. We did it two days in a row. The second time I went with four people from another town. On crossing the river we held on to a rope stretched across the water. We carried our clothes and money in a plastic bag where they would stay dry, but one man, who was afraid that he might lose his grip, let go of his plastic bag, which fell into the river.

A woman, who overheard Delfino tell me his story, told us that she did not have to enter the water because they took her across the river on a raft made of rubber tubes. She was even able to sit all the way. However, that crossing cost her $2,800. Their adventures pale in comparison with Juana who traveled to Houston to be with her husband, Ruben. Her story shows that it could be a real challenge to cross the border, even several decades ago, especially for women with children:

> I tried to cross the border with my daughter who was still a toddler, carrying backpacks full of baby bottles, bottles of milk, crackers, and candy. I did not want my little girl to suffer. We were turned back and made a second attempt to cross. I did not drink water for a whole day—I only took a few small sips when my mouth was too dry. I put lime into my daughter's mouth and fed her some candy whenever I heard her stomach rumbling. I was also robbed. I told my assailants to take all my money, and luckily they did not hurt me. All the time I was praying to God that nothing bad would happen.

In chapter 4 we met Efrain, the boy who got married at age seventeen. In 2009 he traveled to the border with someone who had already learned how to get across. It did not take long to find a skilled coyote; however, the coyote charged $3,000 per person. Efrain and his friend joined a long line of other people and started walking up the side of a steep hill. Efrain, who is skinny, fainted, and his much stronger friend had to carry him for a couple of hours. The friend did not know whether Efrain was dead or alive. Another young man from his hometown was not so lucky and died of dehydration crossing the desert in Arizona. I was living in Mexico when this death occurred, and witnessed the sad spectacle of his father, who had never been to the United States, asking permission to use the telephone in the house where I was staying. He had to arrange for the funeral to be held as soon as his son's body was flown home from the United States. This was the first time someone from that town had died crossing the border, although other people lost their lives in the United States to a serious illness or a car accident. The expression used in those cases is "he came back in a box."

Even when people had a good chance of crossing the border, not everyone was successful, even after several attempts. But the exception has now become the norm. Recently many prospective migrant workers just go back to Guerrero, while others stay near the border. I heard about several such cases: "Every day it is getting more difficult to cross the border. Some have already tried five times and don't have any more money. Some of those who can't get across stay near the border—like Felix's two sons. They are now working as vendors in Tijuana. Manuel and his wife also live near the border."

I have heard about ingenious ways of avoiding border patrols in the past; some waded across shallow sections of the Rio Grand while others clung to the underside of trains as they slowly crossed the border. One man told me he was tied, arms and legs stretched out on both sides, to the top of a cattle truck. Still others took a bus to the border and then passed through a checkpoint using the papers of someone who lives close to the border. They were then put on another bus. However, they almost always had to deal with coyotes. A common image of the coyote, also known as *pollero* (literally, a chicken herder), is that of a human smuggler who takes advantage of people. The media and government officials, including those who work for the U.S. Border Patrol, portray the coyote as an unscrupulous stranger who takes advantage of people he does not know. In contrast, Mexican folk songs represent him as a folk hero who operates outside of the law. The reality is more complex. Since coyotes operate a risky business they cannot provide any guarantees; any customers who are turned back before they reach their destination do not get their money refunded. Yet, up until around 2005, they had a high success rate and were very professional, according to scholars who have done years on research on the phenomenon of *coyotaje* (the practice of smuggling people across the border). The academic literature has revealed that a coyote might well be a friend or a neighbor and that those who were strangers came highly recommended. In the case of the Alto Balsas, I have found both scenarios. In the town where I carried out my survey, most prospective migrants continue to travel to the border to find a coyote someone has recommended; however, in several other towns men who once paid someone to sneak them across the border became coyotes themselves.

A Spanish-speaking man originally born in a small town close to Iguala became the main coyote for several would-be migrants from Maxela, where he had settled after marrying a woman from that village. Soon after he moved to Maxela, in the early seventies, he persuaded several of his new neighbors to let him take them across the border, pointing out that they could earn eight dollars an hour in the United States, instead of the five pesos a day (then worth around five dollars) they earned at home. He charged them three hundred dollars. This coyote also found customers in several Spanish-speaking villages located just outside of the Alto Balsas region, but his most steady customers were not from his new home in Maxela, but from the completely Nahuatl-speaking village of Ahuelican. By the late 1980s men from Ahuelican found another coyote from their own hometown who was fluent in both Spanish and Nahuatl. This new coyote, a man called Federico, had earlier worked in the United States as an illegal immigrant and subsequently benefited from the 1986 amnesty. Like his predecessor from Maxela, Federico personally escorted people from their hometown to Houston. His brother also became a coyote and they took up residence in the border city of Reynosa, but kept in close contact with their father in Ahuelican.

Although migrants who wanted to go to Texas tended to use the services of the coyotes from Ahuelican, anyone headed to California was more likely to first travel to Tijuana by themselves where they would look for a coyote with no connections to their home region. I have heard of only one case in the town where I did my survey where an earlier migrant from that town helped to sneak people who wanted to go to Los Angeles across the border. However, this man, Guillermo, was himself undocumented and was not considered to be a very good coyote. I first heard about this man from someone now living in Los Angeles:

> I know Guillermo, who lives in San Diego. He first helped one of my cousins to cross the border around the same time that I was looking for a coyote in Tijuana. Guillermo, who was once a *bracero*, is from my hometown. He also helped me once and later helped some other *paisanos* (fellow countrymen). We did not have to pay him until later. But I no longer wanted to use him as our coyote because one time he was caught by the *migra* [U.S. Border Patrol guards] and sent back to Mexico. He himself then had to pay another coyote to get back into the U.S.

Not everyone, especially those who have made many border crossings, needs the services of a coyote. Up until recently some men were still able to cross the border successfully without paying a lot of money, as long as they were already very familiar with border procedures and knew how to interact with border officials. These were migrants who had also previously been in the United States and knew the lay of the land. It also helped to have lots of nerve. Toribio, whom we met before, had picked up a bit of English and he was very confident: "The first time I was in the U.S. I bought a car and used that to go back and forth across the border without a coyote. I would just show the border officials my driver's license and say 'I am an American citizen.'" Toribio also tried his hand at human smuggling for a while, although he could only do so by finding American partners:

> When I lived in Houston I was a *pollero*. I would first go back to Mexico to escort men I knew to the border. I would bring them as far as Matamoros where they had to swim across the river on their own. On the other side, in Brownsville, the men would climb into a tanker truck. That is when I would show up again. The owner of that big rig, a *gabacho* [a term used for white Americans], transported gasoline to Houston, but there was room for people in the small compartment behind the driver. You could not see who was in there by looking in from the outside. The people we transported rode standing up; there was room for four but sometimes we could carry up to seven. We thus carried men past two checkpoints and the *migra* were not aware there were men in the space behind the driver.

Toribio had already come to an agreement between the driver and owner of the rig. But another driver, a Chicano who had been one of Toribio's friends, reported what was happening to the authorities when Toribio and the driver did not give him a big enough cut. Consequently they were stopped on their third trip. Toribio recalls: "They were going to detain us, so I started running, as did my guide. But we were caught before we could get back across the river. They deported me and I had to sign a letter saying that I would not come back to the U.S. for five years." Toribio nevertheless continued to cross the border to find work, and came back for visits to see his family once a year, although he gave up on the idea of becoming a professional coyote. When I spoke to him in Mexico in February of 2011 he was planning to go back to the United States as he had done for many years. The fact that an experienced undocumented migrant worker like Toribio has since then not been able to get into the United States shows how it has become much more difficult to cross the border as an undocumented worker. The old ways of getting around the system of border control no longer seem to work and the nature of *coyotaje* itself has changed.

Around the middle of the first decade of this century, the business of bringing people without documents across the U.S. border changed with the increasing presence of drug cartels. For example, Federico and his brother were no longer able to smuggle people from their hometown across the border after a competitor in Reynosa made a deal with someone who had close connections to one of those cartels. He informed the cartel that the two brothers were operating without paying for protection; consequently the two brothers were run out of town. The new cartel coyote in Reynosa does not pick up migrants in Guerrero, nor does he escort them to Houston. The smuggling of illegal migratory workers has taken on a new form involving people in both Mexico and the United States, each in charge of a different leg of the trip. The cartel pays men in several villages in the Alto Balsas region who transport people to a small airport in Cuernavaca, where they board a plane to a city on the border. There someone else provides them with a place to stay until they are ready to be smuggled across. This system, called *cadena* (chain), represents the globalization of organized crime whose tentacles reach into the smallest Mexican hamlets. Nowadays there are few small-scale smuggling entrepreneurs left.

Like anyone who has to deal with a stressful situation, undocumented workers have developed defense mechanisms, including joking to deal with their situation. I overheard one such joke in Isabel's living room, which is always full of visitors. The joke was based on a real story:

> There is this big man from my hometown in Guerrero who was a *mojado* [wetback, a pejorative term referring to Mexican migrants]. They called him Kaime. He is *moreno* [meaning he had dark skin]. He had not been in the U.S. very long but knew a few words of English. One day he went downtown with some friends. They were all illegal migrants. Someone from the *migra* saw him standing by himself and asked him in English, "I heard there are some illegal Mexicans around here. Have you seen any?" Kaime was not sure how to answer or what language he should use. He remained silent for a minute than answered, "Ay dunnoow [I don't know]," using the same way of speaking he had heard American blacks use. That immigration officer just walked away and Kaime's friends were relieved. Later they had a good laugh.

Another joke I have heard many times is that the new wall being built across the border will never be finished because they will not find enough undocumented workers to do the work. Despite the current clampdown on illegal immigrants, the people who tell such jokes are convinced the American government will never be able to halt the influx of undocumented workers.

American government officials initially thought tighter border controls would result in a reversal of the flow of people between the United States and Mexico. This did not happen for more than a decade after the signing of NAFTA. To the contrary, the total numbers of undocumented Mexican workers coming to the United States actually went up after new border restrictions were put in place. Only after 2010 did the clampdown on illegal crossings make a dent in the influx of migrants, at least in the case of the Alto Balsas. Yet even before it became nearly impossible to cross the border, the majority of undocumented Mexicans were already staying in the United States, because they became more reluctant to risk being detained on a return from home visits.

Despite stricter border control and new regulations designed to deter undocumented workers already in the United States, young people born and raised in Mexico have not given up hope; they keep trying to cross the border. In October 2011, when I visited the Nahua town I am most familiar with, I discovered that, of twenty school graduates who traveled to the border that summer, only three reached their final destination. This is a dramatic development since in the past the number of graduates who managed to enter the United States far outweighed those who did not make it across. Yet more than half of the seventeen who failed to enter the United States in the summer of 2011 were planning to make another attempt to cross the border. When I returned in January 2013, they were still planning and hoping and in January of 2014 I heard the news that two of them had finally managed to get across.

Back in the United States undocumented workers tell me they are not worried about being questioned or getting arrested. When I did an interview with Juana, the woman who once had a hard time crossing the border with her daughter, she proclaimed: "I live from day to day and I am not afraid of anyone. I do not worry about the *migra* picking me up; I go wherever I want." Undocumented workers keep telling themselves and others that they are not afraid of being picked up and deported. Yet there is always the lingering doubt about what the future holds in store. Undocumented workers are fully aware of the limitations of their lack of legal status. One man, who now works in construction, lamented: "I have been here for eleven years but I have not gone back. It would be too difficult to reenter the U.S. with the whole family. Before, when I lived in Mexico, I was an *artesano* and free to travel all the way to the state of Sonora to sell my crafts. Here we are all locked in a box and cannot get out."

"In the United States All You Do Is Work"

In the summer of 2006, during a stay in Mexico, I saw a young man talking to a group of workers. He alternately gave them orders, but also joked with them: "Come on, give me a hand." I stopped to introduce myself and found out that he had just arrived to supervise the last stages of the construction of his house. He was going to get married in less than a week. He gave me his name, Alejandro, and bragged that he had spent some time in an American jail, which turned out not to be true. He told me that he had lived in the United States for most of his life, but changed his demeanor after I told him that I knew his parents and where they lived. I later found out that Alejandro had been in the United States for only six years and that he had never been arrested. He and his new bride were staying in his hometown for several months before going back to the United States. I did not attend Alejandro's wedding, which took place a few days after I left town. Instead, I was able to see the festivities by watching a video in their apartment in Atlanta, Georgia, five years later. I was not surprised to see a mix of ancient traditions and a Western-style bridal gown, the banquet, the speeches of village elders, and the live band that provided the music for a dance held on the *cancha*, an outdoor basketball court. I had already observed such weddings in Mexico. What was unique was the groom's costume; instead of a rented tuxedo he wore the uniform of a British naval officer. Alejandro paid five hundred dollars for that outfit because he "wanted to be like a member of the British royal family." He told me he wanted to show his neighbors and relatives: "Look, I am the most important person in the village." I found out that both the bridal gown and his uniform were safely locked away in his house in Mexico, waiting for the village prince to come home.

The bravado and confidence I had so far associated with this young man stands in sharp contrast to his daily life and demeanor in the United States. His experience shows that an undocumented worker can be a somebody in Mexico but a nobody in the United States. Alejandro was lucky to still hold a job in 2011 during a period of high unemployment, but he had to get up early every morning to cut lawns, plant grass, and dig up gardens. He put in long hours and found the work tiring. His wife had just lost her part-time job working in the kitchen of a restaurant. Alejandro told me: "I don't want to get involved in drug trafficking or do anything bad. I just want to work hard to support my wife and my children. I want to send some money to my mother in Mexico."

Each person has his or her own story; the stories I collected illustrate the wide range of jobs held by undocumented workers. It soon became apparent that there are great differences in how they found their first job in the United States, what kind of work they have done, how they got along with coworkers and employers, and whether or not they enjoyed or learned from the job. The common theme is that their lives in the United States revolve around work. Time and time again people talked about whether or not they could work enough days per week and sufficient hours each day to cover their living costs and also save money. Almost everyone commented on how hard they have to work and how stressful the work could be, compared to the more relaxed pace of life in Mexico. At the same time they told me that living in the United States provides them with opportunities to get ahead.

Some migrant workers end up doing the same kind of work and even work for the same employer for a long time but it is more common for undocumented workers to go from job to job. The story of Ruben illustrates the career of an undocumented worker with a more checkered career. He never succeeded in getting a job that lasted for more than four years, and he was still doing part-time work when I visited his home in 2010. In my first interview he started by telling me how he got his first job in the United States:

> At first I lived with two other cousins who told me they knew a man who employed people without documents. I started earning ninety dollars a week doing yard work, but gave my cousins most of what I earned to pay for my share of the rent, food and other expenses. I would only have fifteen dollars left at the end of each week, which was not much to send home to my wife.

Like many newcomers, Ruben had to start at the bottom, with a low-paid, part-time job, until he could find more permanent employment. However, he was at a disadvantage because he had not brought his Mexican birth certificate needed to apply for better jobs. Ruben sent a power of attorney to his wife, which enabled her to get a new copy issued and sent to her husband. With that, plus an address of where he was staying, he had no trouble getting an American identification card (he did not tell me what kind of card it was). That was back in 1978. Ruben told me how he got a better job after getting that card: "My first job was for Fiesta, a chain of big department stores. I got that job with my identification card, plus a recommendation, and started earning a minimum wage of $3.22 an hour, doing shelving. I had to move heavy boxes, which was hard work."

It is not unusual for an undocumented worker to be asked to do a variety of jobs, sometimes in more than once location, even if it might take longer, or require a car to get there. Ruben started off using a bicycle to get to work, but eventually he had to buy car since he worked in Houston, which is a sprawling city without an underground transportation system. Not having a car in Houston puts undocumented workers at a disadvantage. One needs a car to move around quickly when applying for multiple jobs and to get to work once you have a job that is not in the downtown core or far away from where one lives: "When freeway 10 was built, I was transferred to a Fiesta store on Mason Street, and I got several raises until I reached the maximum of $7.75. There I also did shelving, until they asked me to clean floors, using a machine to apply wax and then polish. I worked a full-time, eight-hour night shift, from 11 p.m. until seven in the morning."

Like many undocumented workers working for larger companies, an ID was not sufficient by itself. Ruben's friends helped him to obtain other documents, such as a Social Security number and proof of legal entry into the United States, but some of those papers were false. Even the managers of large companies at that time were willing to turn a blind eye, and helped the people they wanted to hire with false documents. But working with false papers is also a great excuse to fire workers. Ruben lamented: "I lost that job with Fiesta in September of 1997 and I did not have steady work for almost a year. Instead I helped people with moving and cutting lawns. I was paid in cash and used to earn $4.25 an hour. My wife cleaned houses." Regardless of the size of the firm, getting a job, even a part-time one, still requires a recommendation. After a year of sporadic employment, Ruben met someone from his home state of Guerrero:

One day, at a party, I spoke to a man from my home state who worked as a janitor in a retirement home. When he found out I knew how to handle a floor polisher, he told me that they had an emergency in his place of employment, that they needed someone who knows how to clean floors. That work lasted for almost two years, until I got laid off in 2009, on the first of May. Since then I have been doing odd jobs.

Two years later, when I did my second interview with Ruben, he told me that his best part-time job was cleaning and polishing the floor of an exercise gym, earning the minimum wage of $7.25 an hour. This undocumented worker, the man with a diploma in accounting whom we met in the first chapter, is unique because he had already lived and worked in Mexico City before moving to Houston. He is also better educated than other men of his generation.

Toribio, whom we met in chapter 2, had more luck in finding jobs in the United States even though he only had a third-grade education:

I know Houston quite well because I worked there for five years in a restaurant called Denny's. I had a lot of friends there who are from Ahuelican. I left Houston to work in construction in Ontario, California, since I could earn more money there. In Houston they paid me 270 dollars per week but in Ontario I earned six hundred dollars and more if I worked on Saturdays. After Ontario I went to Los Angeles for a year and a half. There I again worked in Denny's, based on a recommendation from my former boss in Houston.

Although he is an undocumented worker, Toribio was able to go back and forth between the United States and Mexico without too much hassle until recently. Whenever he was in the United States, he lived like a bachelor, but made sure his wife and children were provided for. "When I was working in California I had everything figured out. Half of my earning was for my family in Mexico and the rest for my living costs—gasoline, food, and rent. What was left over, like maybe 150 dollars, was for my own enjoyment." Toribio told me about the kinds of work he did in various jobs. It became clear that he did not like all of the jobs he had held, especially if his boss was too demanding. Whenever he is back in Mexico, Toribio has more leisure time but also does a bit of work, as we saw in the chapter where I talked about undocumented workers who are artisans when they return to Mexico. In the United States all Toribio does is work.

Working as an illegal immigrant in the American underground economy is not easy and one has to be willing to take whatever job becomes available. One problem is that most employers do not provide job training. So if undocumented workers want to learn the skills necessary to move into better-paid positions, they have to learn on their own. We can use the textile industry as an example. Most of the people who went to Los Angeles had no prior training in sewing, yet this industry was one of the only sources of employment for undocumented workers in that city. So they had to adapt. Bulfrano told me: "I came here in 1994 and started working in a textile factory. My first job there was trimming, cutting off all the loose threads from clothes that had already been sewn together. After a while I started working with an ironing board. I did that for two years, but I wanted to work with a sewing machine where one can earn more." Bulfrano did not know how to sew so he took lessons in a private night school founded by a former employee who had bought his own sewing machines. The school consisted of a room where its founder, also its sole teacher, had installed his machines. Bulfrano paid seventy-four dollars a week to that teacher, but found it difficult to learn how to sew there. Several months later Bulfrano asked the lady for whom he worked to let him try working on a sewing machine. But he was still not good enough. He was told, "You don't know how to sew," and he lost his job. Bulfrano gave me his theory about why textile factories in Los Angeles do not provide job training: "They are afraid that if they teach you how to sew well, you will just go and work somewhere else. That is what happened with my uncle once he knew his job really well."

Bulfrano started looking for, and managed to find, a textile factory where the type of sewing required for the job was not as difficult to learn. It was a job that consisted of sewing together sections of pants made from very thick fabric. It was slow work but every day he could do it better. But that job still did not pay that well, so through the recommendations of some friends he got a job in yet another factory. There Bulfrano learned how to sew together the middle sections of short-sleeved shirts. He became quite good at it and his wages jumped to a higher level. However, he was not able to put in the hours he needed since that kind of work did not keep him busy all day. He could have asked to be transferred to another department but instead he quit and found another job that better matched his skill level, and where he could also work longer hours:

> I did not want to put on sleeves or collars in the place where I was working because that would have taken me too long to learn—I would not be able to earn as much money because I would not have been able to work fast enough. So I went to yet another factory where they had more work that I could already do quickly. For two years I was able to pick up a lot of work and sometimes I would not come home until early in the evening.

Bulfrano's wife, Ofelia, also works in the fashion district of downtown Los Angeles. She told me quite a different story about how she learned to sew and get steady work:

> I like working as a seamstress. Like other workers, I started off doing only trimming and did that for two years. One day the lady who is my boss asked me if I wanted to do something different; she wanted to know if I would like to use a sewing machine. I told her I had never used a sewing machine but she gave me a chance to learn by starting with sewing something simple. She showed me what to do and let me to practice on my own time. I did not have to go to a sewing school like my husband.

Not only did Ofelia have a more accommodating boss, she was much better at operating more complex, advanced sewing machines. She had no trouble finding a better-paying job after a couple of years:

> Learning how to sew was like learning how to drive a car. It can be nerve wracking at first but I soon became more confident and it became second nature. I learned quickly and can now work with different kinds of machines,

some of which allow you to do more complicated tasks like double stitching. My specialty is sewing up the edges of sleeves and collars, stitching both sides after doubling up the fabric.

Angelina, who came to the United States when she was fifteen, had to learn a very different kind of job in Texas. Like other undocumented workers Angelina does not receive extra pay for working overtime, nor does she receive holiday pay, although in her case she did get on-the-job training:

> My first job was looking after children in peoples' homes and I also worked as a cleaner in a hospital. That was before I started working in a donut shop that is part of a chain. The person who later became my husband was already working here. They taught me how to become a cashier at one of their larger stores where they do all their training. It did not matter that I knew little English. I was one of the first women from my town to work there.

Although many undocumented workers from the Alto Balsas are employed in the service sector, others, including women, have jobs that are physically more demanding. Jessica, who currently lives in California, has a job in a plant nursery. I first met her in her Mexican hometown in the winter of 2006 when she and her husband, Juan, had come home for a visit. I overheard her telling her mother-in-law about her job in the United States while showing the scars on her knees from kneeling down while grafting plants: "I get paid fifty dollars for every thousand plants; it is possible to do up to three thousand per day which enables a worker to earn almost two thousand dollars in a two-week period. It is hard work." I spoke to her again in November 2011 when I stayed at their house in California. Jessica drove me to the nursery where she works but the staff who work at the front desk of the company's office would not give me permission to enter so I could not observe the kind of work she does. But the next day she told me all about what she does and her work conditions:

> Today I finished at three in the afternoon because there was not as much work. But next Monday I have to work for nine hours, from seven in the morning until four in the afternoon. Sometimes, when I arrive at work early in the morning, I don't have a plastic sheet to protect me from the moisture. That is why I had to go and buy rubber boots and raingear the other day. And they give us different tasks. For example, the other day I

washed out containers and you have to know what you are doing. Last week
we planted walnuts and next week we will cut off the top part of each plant
when they get grafted.

When I started to investigate the ethnic composition of the workplaces
of undocumented workers, I also found considerable variation. In some
cases, the workforce consists entirely of Spanish-speaking people, including those from other countries in Latin America. Supervisors, managers,
and in some cases even owners, all spoke Spanish. But in most cases, there
were both Mexican undocumented and native-born English-speaking
workers, including whites, as in the big plant nursery where Jessica works.
Consequently she, as did several other Spanish-speaking employees, had
to learn a bit of English. In contrast, some workplaces had mainly undocumented workers and in some cases most of those workers came from
the same town in the Alto Balsas, as I discovered when I paid a visit to the
back section of a donut shop in Houston where most of the work gets done.
When I arrived at five in the morning I observed three women cleaning
and then putting the finished donuts on a tray on a wheeled cart. They
later served customers while their husbands were busy making donuts; I
saw one of the men taking a tray of donuts and placing it in a vat of hot oil
to cook, and later, in another tray, applying a coat of sugar in one stroke.
The donuts are then placed on two conveyor belts.

It is not common for husbands and wives, both undocumented, to work
for the same employer. For most couples, the man and the woman both
have jobs, although they rarely work for the same boss. This was the case
for Jessica and Juan. Their work lives are quite separate, unlike husbands
and wives from the Alto Balsas who all work closely together in the craft
industry or the maize fields. Yet in the United States older children who
are not yet married also pitch in just as they do in Mexico. For example,
Juan and Jessica's eighteen-year-old son got a part-time job working for
the same landscape firm as his father. He hands over part of his paycheck
to his mother, but he is allowed to keep part of what he earns to buy the
video games he likes playing on their television at home. This couple sends
money to Juan's parents in Mexico, but only when there is enough work.
Such remittances have become an important second source of income for
many people in their home region. Occasional Western Union money
transfers to parents in Mexico do not go a long way, but more substantial

remittances sent for house construction represent a major infusion of cash into the economy of the Alto Balsas.

The size of remittances for any individual or couple varies over their lifespan. A young person recently arrived in the United States usually does not send home much, if any, money at first, even if they have a job waiting for them. He or she first needs to pay off the loan used to pay the coyote. Such loans are usually given by a relative or a friend already living in the United States. It takes anywhere from several months to two years to pay off the cost of one's passage, including the coyote. At that point the remittances can start flowing; I have heard about young, unmarried women being able to send home the ten or twenty thousand dollars needed to build a new family home within five years, not including additional money for miscellaneous expenditures or emergencies. But as soon as a young migrant starts his or her own family, he or she will no longer be able to contribute a lot to the maintenance of elderly parents and other relatives in Mexico. In all cases the money, normally sent to a parent or older sibling once a month, is sent in smaller amounts. Such remittances allow people in Mexico to order building supplies and pay the wages of a bricklayer and his assistants. Another kind of remittance consists of money sent only during the peak period of the agricultural cycle in Mexico to cover the cost of fertilizer, insecticides, and the cost of day laborers. In 2010 five thousand pesos (less than five hundred dollars) was enough grow the maize required for the consumption needs of a small family. In contrast, the cost of a baptism, wedding, or *quinceañera* (celebration of a girl's fifteenth birthday) in Mexico can become quite substantial. For example, the cost just for a live band of musicians can run to ten thousand pesos (a little less than a thousand dollars). Even if other people help to pay for the costs of such events, people working in the United States still have to save up for many years. That is why young couples do not return to a hometown in Mexico for a wedding until after at least ten years of living together in the United States. Once they return to the United States they have to start saving money again, to cover the cost of the *quinceañera* of a daughter. If you are good at handling money, you might be able to save additional money to retire, preferably in rural Mexico where one does not have to spend a lot of money.

One way that some people supplement their income is to make extra money selling such products as cosmetics, footwear, or food supplements in their spare time. It did not take too long for undocumented workers to learn about network marketing companies like Amway. One needs a car to get around to visit clients and some start-up money. Officially they are not employees, but self-employed owners of small businesses who then recruit other people to also sell. They earn income from the retail markup on products they sell personally plus a bonus based on the sales volume of other vendors one has recruited. Antonio, a young man whom we will meet again in chapter 8, worked his way up the Amway ladder, selling nutritional supplements and recruiting others for over ten years. However, Antonio is somewhat exceptional. He worked his way up from textile worker to manager of a textile factory and also founded an amateur band. Others find that selling products is not really worth the effort. Ofelia, the textile worker we have already met, told me about the rewards and risks associated with selling shoes for an international company called Andreas:

> I find my own clients and leave a catalog at someone's home for them to look at for a couple of days. I then go and pick up their shoes at the Andreas' outlet to deliver to their door. One does not earn much, only 9 percent. Some clients, who want more expensive shoes, pay in installments but I have to pay upfront to the company. It is like a business. Other vendors charge their clients interest—but not me! My friends and I only sell to people we know well, like neighbors and relatives. Another lady sells to people in the factory where she works but that is risky, especially if you extend credit, because clients may leave the factory and no one knows where they have gone. I still have a few clients but a lot less than before because it is a lot of extra work and I am tired. The main advantage of staying in this line of work, and buying new catalogs each month, is that I can sell footwear at a reduced price, like the sandals for my husband that you saw me pick up the other day.

Undocumented workers are able to make a small profit working with such marketing companies by tapping into their extensive social networks of people from their own hometown. It is more convenient for undocumented workers who do not own cars and for women tied up with very small children at home to buy from a trusted *paisano*. Those who sell these products usually have some prior experience as craft vendors in Mexico. However, they do not find it an easy way to earn money and not everyone can afford the initial capital needed to get started.

Given the challenges involved in achieving a reasonable standard of living while also fulfilling expected duties to a hometown, there is not much room to save up the money needed to set up a small business in Mexico. But a few people have managed to do so. One way to invest money and get some returns in the long run is to buy cattle. This kind of investment requires that someone back home is willing to occasionally keep an eye on the beef cattle or goats that will graze in the open shrubland of the village lands not suitable for cultivation. It does not make any sense to buy pigs or chickens if you are not yourself living in Mexico because they require a lot of care and attention. But that is an option for when one goes back to Mexico to retire. A few migrant workers have built cement water tanks and arranged to put up fences to set up a small ranch but that is only possible if you own some land with a source of water. A more common and viable business in rural Mexico is to turn part of your house into a small variety store, as long as you have a wife or a parent there to serve customers. Every town in the Alto Balsas region has a half dozen such stores that sell pop and candies. The steady customers are schoolchildren with money originating from remittances. Building more houses would not make any sense, because no one in the Alto Balsas needs to rent the house where they live. But one could generate income in Mexico by buying a vehicle used to transport goods and people. I know of many men, and one woman, who have brought back a van or a pickup truck for that purpose. We have already seen how some undocumented workers with experience in the craft industry have used the money they earned in the United States to become full-time vendors, but such an investment can be risky, given the competitive nature of that industry.

How much money is sent home, as opposed to how much is spent in the United States, can fluctuate wildly. It depends on the amount of money earned, as well as needs in Mexico. For example, Juan and Jessica, who have five children to support in the United States, send several hundred dollars to Mexico whenever Juan's mother needs to pay for medication injected by a private doctor when her leg is hurting too much. In 2007 they paid much of the cost for the funeral of Cristobal, Juan's older brother who did not have children of his own. In 2009 they paid for Cristobal's widow to have a cataract operation that was not covered by Mexico's health care system. In each case three or four thousand dollars were transferred to a bank in the city of Iguala. Each money transfer usually includes the extra twenty dollars required to pay for the fare needed to take a van to Iguala. And undocumented workers will be expected to still send remittances to support hometown festivities, including elaborate fireworks displays. To cover the costs of all these culturally expected contributions in one's hometown, much less saving up money to set up a small business in Mexico, means that both men and women have to work long hours as migrant workers to earn the money they need. Poor relatives at home might consider all undocumented workers in the United States to be very well off, especially if those migrants have been away for a long time. But that is usually not the case. Irineo, who has spent most of the last twenty years in San Diego, was still struggling to cover the costs of renting a very modest home and of supporting his five children, three of whom were born in the United States. His wife, who is no longer working, looks after his elderly father, who had recently lost his sight. His children had paid for an expensive operation for advanced diabetes, which allowed him to live a few years longer, but this did not prevent him from becoming completely blind. When I visited him in November of 2013, Irineo told me, "we are not rich." Being an undocumented worker in the United States is not easy. Those whom I know are generally upbeat and optimistic, but they sometimes wonder whether or not they have made the right choice. Not everyone thinks that working in the United States is such a great idea. Pablo, the craft vendor now living in Cuernavaca, whom we met in chapter 2, decided he would rather not work in the United States: "I enjoy living in Mexico. I work a bit but I can also take it easy. In the U.S. all you do is work and work and work. When there is no work, you cannot pay your bills. You can never relax."

"For Me It Is about the Same"

Migrant workers from the Alto Balsas can be found all over the United States, although most ended up in Texas and California. The majority of people from Ahuelican went to Houston, starting as early as the seventies. Most of the migrants from San Miguel Tecuiciapan also went to Houston, where they live in other parts of the city than those from Ahuelican. More recent migrants from towns with close links to Ahuelican, such as Ostotipan, Totoltsintlan, and San Agustin Oapan, ended up in the same neighborhoods of Houston as those of Ahuelican. Some people from Ahuehuepan live in another part of Houston. In contrast, migrants from the predominantly Spanish-speaking towns of Maxela and Xalitla live and work in Ontario, California, as do most people from the still completely Nahuatl-speaking town of San Juan Tetelcingo. People from Xalitla, Ahuehuepan, and many other towns originally worked, or still work, in downtown Los Angeles. Some people from these and other towns also reside in other urban centers of California such as Sacramento and San Diego. Although the majority of the Nahua population can be found in either Texas or California, migrants from some of the towns already mentioned can be found in Atlanta, Georgia, with a minority going to cities in several other, mainly southern, U.S. states. In any large metropolitan region in that part of the United States one is bound to encounter a few migrants from almost every town in the Alto Balsas region. A few went as far north as Chicago. The common denominator is an urban destination. With the exception of Los Angeles, where all Nahuas live and work downtown, migrants generally reside in the suburbs or in small towns on the edges of large metropolitan centers. For example, I am not aware of anyone living or working anywhere close to the center of Sacramento; rather they congregate in places such as Lincoln, Rancho Cordoba, or Roseville.

In all locations, including Los Angeles, the first to arrive rented apartments or townhouses located on the same street. At first, as many as eight men might have shared a one- or two-bedroom unit, but as whole families settled in the United States, migrants moved further afield, resulting in a more dispersed settlement pattern. Over time, bigger families rented detached houses, although one or two relatives usually moved in temporarily. In a few exceptional cases, people raised money for a mortgage to become first-time homeowners in the United States. Yet most newcomers still start off living in the same locations where the first migrants used to congregate. Regardless of where they end up, migrants know where everyone else from their own hometown lives, and those who live in the same city regularly visit each other. In places where migrants from different towns in Guerrero ended up in the same city, people tend to only come into contact and socialize with people from their home villages, although a few people from different towns in Mexico do sometimes share rides or attend the same parties.

Once they have settled down, people do not tend to move to other parts of a city, much less to another state, although they will make longer trips to visit close friends or relatives. For example, people from one town in the Alto Balsas, who are as likely to live in Los Angeles as the Sacramento area, regularly travel by car between these cities to attend parties to celebrate birthdays or baptisms. However, they never visit anyone, even close relatives, living in the San Diego area, including small towns north of San Diego, because of the higher risk of being stopped at the immigration checkpoints located along the highways between San Diego and Los Angeles. Likewise, the half dozen families with undocumented workers from the Alto Balsas region who have settled down in this part of California rarely dare to travel farther north. In contrast, undocumented workers who were already well established in Los Angeles did not hesitate to relocate their families to Sacramento during a period of increasing unemployment in the L.A. area textile industry after 9/11. Occasionally, someone might move to a different city or even state for personal reasons, as in the case of Paula who moved from California to Texas to live with another brother.

Since almost everyone will have either moved or knows someone from their hometown who lives in other locations, undocumented workers invariably make comparisons. Each destination has its own advantages and disadvantages, and the people I interviewed gave me different reasons for moving. My conversations made me aware that working conditions, the cost of living, wages, and the availability of public services vary between states, as well as between cities within the same state. Venancio, a man who offered me a ride in Guerrero in 2010, spoke to me about the relative merits of different destinations when we spoke at length while driving to the city of Iguala:

> I work as a cabinet maker in Atlanta. There are around twenty of us [from my hometown] in that city, mainly working in roofing. I am the only one working as a carpenter. I first went to the U.S. when I was twenty years old, to work in Los Angeles in a textile factory. But I don't like using a sewing machine and would rather work outside. That is why I moved to Georgia. I was also in Ontario [California] where my brothers are working. One does framing for houses and the other works for Big Burger. He started off working in Georgia before moving to Lincoln but he did not like Georgia; he encountered racism there, more than in Texas or California. But I like Georgia.

Venancio is undocumented but he did have a valid American driver's license at the time I spoke to him, so we ended up talking about the implications of driving in different states. He told me that undocumented workers in Georgia who are caught driving without a license are given a two-year jail sentence and must also pay a fine. But at least their cars are not confiscated and they would not be automatically deported, which was then the case in California.

During my visits to the United States, undocumented workers told me how the availability of public services, as well as housing policies, also influenced choices about where to stay. Gaudencio said:

> I do not have any health insurance, but here in Houston they will still attend to you in the emergency wards of hospitals. That is not the case in other states. One of our friends was refused treatment and came to Houston just for that reason. We know lots of *paisanos* (fellow countrymen) who recently moved here because it is easier for them to work and live in Texas.

Juan, who lives in the Sacramento area, drew my attention to a recent change in one city's laws that will deter more undocumented workers:

> Right now I drive here without a license, but I remember how it used to be easy to just invent a Social Security number to get a license because they did not use computers to check if that number was real or not. That is no longer possible, plus governments are getting stricter all the time about how Social Security cards get used. In San Diego you can no longer rent an apartment without a proper Social Security number. At least that is not the case here in Sacramento.

When I started doing interviews in California, I found out that the experiences of undocumented workers differ quite a bit even within that state. Tomas thought it was better to live in the Sacramento area because one could earn more money working in landscaping or construction than if you worked in the textile district of Los Angeles. But someone else pointed out that it costs less to live in Los Angeles, because rents for apartments were lower and textile workers are not as dependent on cars to get to work. In the Sacramento area it is difficult and very time consuming for families to get by without a car for shopping and getting to work. Hilario, who spent several years living in California, told me:

> In the Sacramento area, people from Ahuehuepan live in several small towns close to Sacramento itself, and they do visit each other quite often. They all drive because to go by bus, both within and between those towns, would take a long time. Those buses are really slow. It is very different in Los Angeles where there are many bus lines that take you downtown very quickly and most people who work in the textile factories live close to downtown.

Undocumented workers who live in the small towns and suburbs of the Sacramento area have to earn enough money to buy a car and pay for its upkeep. In contrast, less than a third of the Nahua families from Guerrero in Los Angeles own a car; they can easily get around by bus, which cost only $1.50 per ride in 2012. One person told me that having a car in Los Angeles is a luxury, not a necessity. Los Angeles also has other advantages: "In Los Angeles there are lots of bars and dance halls where you can meet other Latinos. Here in Lincoln there are no clubs for Latinos. Well, it is true there is a club, but it is more exclusive and you need to buy a membership. They would not like outsiders to join. None of us ever goes there." Yet I have also heard people say that the advantage of staying in a smaller city or living in the suburbs of places like Sacramento is that one gets more exposure to English both at work and on the street, which makes it more likely you will pick it up. They made the observation that migrants living in places like downtown Los Angeles only hear and use Spanish, and that they only associate with other Latinos.

Another basis of comparison is the nature of jobs held. Most men from the Alto Balsas prefer to work in landscaping or yard maintenance although the only job open to them in Los Angeles is working in a textile factory. However, personal preferences vary. For example, I found out that Cirilo actually prefers to work in Los Angeles: "I have been in Ontario, where I did garden work, cutting grasses and trimming trees, but I don't like that work and could not always finish what I was doing. I prefer to work with a sewing machine. I have no trouble completing the work they give me in Los Angeles."

Although migrant families with children in the United States may sometimes move to another location after staying in one place for several years, it is not likely that they will move back to that place if both the husband and wife are successful in finding relatively stable employment. I was thus surprised to discover, during my third trip to California, that Bulfrano and Ofelia had at one point moved the whole family to Sacramento for eight months, after assuming that they had always worked in textile factories in Los Angeles. They moved there in the mid-nineties when Bulfrano had been invited to move to the Sacramento area to work in landscaping, where he could earn more money doing something he enjoyed doing. However, Ofelia, who had always earned more as a skilled seamstress in the textile industry, found out that she could not earn even half of what she was paid in Los Angeles in her new job in a dry cleaning business. Since she had previously been able to earn more per hour than her husband, their total family income went down, while their cost of living increased. The main benefit of their stay in Sacramento is that they both learned how to drive and brought a car they bought there back to Los Angeles.

Based on a limited number of interviews and observations in several locations, I would not hazard to come up with conclusions about which type of work or location would be the most advantageous for undocumented indigenous workers in urban settings. Such workers would probably find such a question of little relevance, given that their main preoccupation is that they are undocumented and that they all work in the lower end of the job market. Those who work as cashiers or waiters, jobs that require a better knowledge of English, still do not earn that much more. But at least their employment is more secure than working in the more volatile construction sector of the economy, which is more sensitive to fluctuations in the economy. Regardless of the relative merits of some jobs over others, undocumented workers have accepted that they have to take what they can get, and hope that their boss will treat them well. The best way to summarize people's preferences is to use the words of Heleodoro:

> I first came to Los Angeles to work in a textile factory. In 1995 I moved to Lincoln [California] where I have been working in landscaping. The advantage of working in a textile factory is that you can work and earn money even when it is raining, which is not the case in landscaping. Even though a person earns less sewing in a factory, the living costs are also less. But you usually end up working longer hours. Here in Lincoln most people get off from work at three o'clock in the afternoon, so if you wanted you could take on another job. Right now there is not much work here in the Sacramento area but I am not going to return to Los Angeles because my children are already going to school here. For me working in Lincoln or working in Los Angeles or any other place in the U.S. is about the same.

The undocumented workers that I got to know in the United States were generally not familiar with government agencies or worker-run worker centers (and they were not aware there were different kinds of worker centers). But those who did know about such services did not hesitate to use them when required. For example, a group of workers in one textile factory in Los Angeles contacted the state Labor Commission to report that their boss had refused to pay what he owed them. When I asked if they were aware that there are worker centers that can help immigrant workers, they told me they have no use for them. One man pointed out that in the case of Los Angeles a restaurant such as McDonald's hires only documented workers, because there are already lots of documented Latino workers. They pointed out that in smaller towns outside of Sacramento, with fewer people, undocumented workers from the Alto Balsas had no problem getting a job at McDonald's because they did not have to compete with documented Latinos. Hence they do not need a worker center. When I asked about what contacts Nahua undocumented workers had with government labor agencies, or community-based worker centers in other big cities, I was told, "None at all; we are on our own."

8

"MEXICANS ARE GOOD WORKERS"

In July of 2007, a cab driver in Houston who is originally from Nigeria told me: "If I want anyone to do a job for me, like cut the lawn or to help with moving, I will ask a Mexican. They are the best workers and you can always rely on them." This cab driver's comment is consistent with the observations of ethnographic studies that report that undocumented workers from Mexico are highly regarded. In a case study of busboys who work in a restaurant in Chicago, Gomberg-Muñoz reports that they are considered by their employer to be "the best workers we have." However, not everyone holds this view. Some native-born Americans vilify Mexican undocumented workers as criminals because they are "illegal," and even those who admire their work ethnic may express the racist opinion that Mexican migrants are suitable only for manual labor and low-status jobs. At the same time, people who have a favorable and less stereotyped opinion of Mexican workers can be ambivalent about the perceived willingness of those workers to work hard without complaining.

In February 2011, when I was heading back to the airport in Los Angeles in a taxi, the cab driver, a white American, started talking about the Mexicans he got to know when working for a large construction firm. He told me that the other workers used to complain that Mexicans worked too fast, but also mentioned that his former boss would not have been able to stay in business if he suddenly lost all of his Mexican workers. On other occasions I sensed Mexican workers were resented by coworkers as rate busters, that is, as people who would take work for lower wages and thus lower the wage rate for other workers. These opinions need to be critically examined in light of the long history of Mexican workers in the United States, what motivates Mexican workers to take what Americans consider to be low-paying, menial, or difficult jobs, and how undocumented workers need to conform to the image that they are hard workers in order to have a competitive advantage in the labor market.

It is easy to understand why American blue-collar workers, many of whom have lost benefits and the protection of strong unions, feel threatened by the influx of undocumented workers willing to work for minimum or less than minimum wages. People brought up in a country like the United States, with a good standard of living and high expectations, expect to earn at least as much as their parents. But in today's global economy, Americans with few specialized skills are at a competitive disadvantage compared to undocumented workers who seem eager to accept jobs without benefits. At the same time, employers who must compete in the global economy need access to cheap labor to stay in business. That is why they prefer to employ undocumented immigrant workers who are vulnerable and hence less likely to complain or quit their jobs. From the perspective of labor unions American employers are exploiting Mexican workers, who have little bargaining power. From the perspective of migrant workers those employers are giving them the jobs they need to meet their goals in life. Those jobs might not be ideal, but they do allow migrants to buy what they could not afford in Mexico, as well as to raise their families and save up some money.

One cannot understand the motivation of migrants, and why they cross the border without documents, without taking into account the lack of viable economic prospects in Mexico. Unemployment is high and the pay is abysmal compared to even the least desirable jobs in the United States. The photojournalist David Bacon has pointed out that a worker with a manufacturing job in Mexico in 1975 earned 23 percent of his American counterpart, and only one-eighth as much for a similar job in the United States in

2002. In most of rural Mexico there are no decent jobs at all. Between 1975 and 2002, the buying power of American workers went down, but that of Mexican workers declined even more. Moreover, what is considered to be an adequate income or a decent wage is relative, and depends on what people consider to be basic needs. Those needs, including consumer goods such as cell phones or televisions that were once luxuries, have changed even in Mexico, but the gap between what people need and what they can afford is much greater in Mexico. Consequently, wages considered at least adequate, and sometimes even generous, from the viewpoint of a Mexican migrant are considered too low by Americans. Migrants are used to getting along with less, which explains why even undocumented workers earning low wages can accumulate enough capital to set up a small business or build a house in Mexico. The ability of Mexican migrants to have some money left over seems almost miraculous to Americans who are having a hard time just meeting what they consider basic necessities. According to Judith Hellman, in order to understand why undocumented workers with low-paying jobs manage to get ahead, one should keep in mind that the kind of Mexican migrants interviewed by researchers are more ambitious than the average Mexican, including those who want to work in the United States. They have persevered. Anyone who could not endure the hardships and homesickness associated with living in an often hostile environment in the United States would have long ago gone home.

Given the choice between very low pay or no job at all versus what they consider to be much higher wages, it makes more sense for a person from a depressed rural area or a small town in Mexico to opt for working hard and to take jobs they sometimes don't like. In the jargon used in the business community, undocumented Mexicans constitute a flexible work force. The same thing could be said for all migrant workers in large cities with a multicultural mix of newcomers from other parts of the world that may have an even lower standard of living than Mexico. Many other migrant workers have to send home remittances. What makes Mexicans more noticeable is their sheer numbers; they number in the millions rather than the hundreds or thousands of undocumented workers from other counties. Many Americans would not know that the cleaner or kitchen helper whom they think is a Mexican actually comes from Guatemala or El Salvador.

Mexican undocumented workers have an advantage over migrant workers from other countries because many Americans are already used to thinking of Mexicans as an ideal cheap as well as reliable labor force. In chapter 1 we saw how they were preferred workers going back to the early 1920s, even though Mexicans were at the same time segregated and subject to racial stereotyping as simple-minded people perfectly suited for low-paying and physically demanding and dirty jobs. In her study of busboys in Chicago, Ruth Gomberg-Muñoz noticed that the workers in her study use existing stereotypes to help promote a reputation for themselves as hard workers eager to please their employers, which makes it more likely that they will be hired. In the workplace, these migrants exert peer pressure on their Mexican coworkers to live up to that reputation. Gomberg-Muñoz points out that this strategy of promoting their reputation as hard workers may help them get jobs, but it also reproduces the subordination of all undocumented migrants and other vulnerable members of the workforce in the restaurant business and elsewhere.

To fully understand the situation of undocumented migrants from the Alto Balsas, we need to take into consideration the conditions of their employment, including the complex and sometimes ambiguous relations between these migrant workers and their employers. The undocumented workers with whom I spoke had worked for both big firms and small entrepreneurs; these employers represent qualitatively different experiences. Relations with the owners of small businesses or private individuals are more personal, but may be fraught with misunderstanding and strife as well as acts of kindness and generosity. Big firms run by a huge white collar bureaucracy often seem unpredictable; the fate of undocumented workers can be determined as much by head-office decisions as by the whim of a manager or even a coworker. We have already seen how Ruben worked for a large corporation until he lost his job and had to take on part-time work. He later worked for another big company and also lost that job. Ruben recalls:

> In 1998 I got a job for Kroger's [grocery store chain], which I got by showing the same papers I had earlier been told were no good. It was the same work I had earlier done at Fiesta, but during the day; again I worked long hours. I worked there for five years until they threw me out and for the same reason, not having the right documentation. For the next two years I had occasional part-time jobs.

Ruben did not understand how he could lose a job in a big company yet get hired by another big company with the same papers. His experience illustrates that a willingness to work long hours does not prevent migrant workers from dismissal when employers no longer need them. Yet such employers do not hesitate to hire more Mexicans, even if they are undocumented.

The way undocumented workers get paid constitutes another form of abuse and subterfuge; this can take many forms. Most of the larger companies pay their employees with checks. By law, they have to make deductions for taxes and Social Security. Jessica, the woman working in a plant nursery (see chapter 6), is not sure how her employer manages to keep her on their payroll. Neither she nor the other workers from her hometown have any documents that allow them to work, nor do the others, but they do have Social Security numbers that were obtained for them by their employer. Angelina, the woman who works in a donut shop, is also paid with a check with deductions taken out for taxes and Social Security. The company she works for pays in cash for any hours beyond the total in the check, but in each case she earns $7.70 per hour and cannot expect a raise. Gomberg-Muñoz reports a somewhat similar situation in a restaurant in Chicago where the payroll department issues biweekly checks with deductions for the first forty hours of work, and a check with no deductions from another account for overtime hours, but without paying time and a half as required by law. In the case of Ruben, who worked for a retirement home in Houston for two years, he was always paid with checks, never cash, and did not know how his employer did it. His boss was aware that he was an undocumented worker but knew how to get around the law. Other, usually smaller, employers only pay cash under the table.

American employers tap into the well-established networks of friends, neighbors, and relatives of undocumented workers in order to recruit any additional workers they need, and to assure that they can always find replacements when necessary. This is why they prefer to hire migrants who are related, or who come from the same town in Mexico. When Paula drove me around Houston to show where her many cousins are living, she told me that they all work for the same chain of donut shops. They are all members of two large extended families in her hometown. The men all work as bakers and the women as cashiers. Migrants, in turn, know that having workers from the same small town in Mexico is advantageous to American employers.

Angelina, the first woman to be hired by this chain, provides further insights into why employers prefer undocumented workers who know each other and belong to a close-knit social circle of people with the same ethnic background: "The bosses know that we are good workers so they ask us who else should be hired. The company, which owns many stores, employs a lot of people but most of the workers they used to hire stayed for a short while and then left. They know that the people from my hometown are going to stay for a long time." I asked Angelina whether she and her co-workers were allowed to take unpaid holidays or to miss work if they got sick: "Yes, it is possible to get permission to take time off work. In my case I told them I would be away for two months for my wedding in Mexico but that I would return. They know I will always find a replacement." The only drawback for employers is that such workers often dictate who else will be hired. If a regular worker has to take time off work, an undocumented worker will simply tell the manager whom to hire as a replacement. This is what happened with Paula, the cashier mentioned earlier. She got her job through her cousin, much to the chagrin of the head office who did not like the fact that they were losing control over hiring. Jacqueline Maria Hagan, who conducted a study of a Mayan community in Houston, observed similar control over the supply and allocation of labor by indigenous migrants.

Often people from the same hometown may constitute only a small portion of workers, especially in workplaces that have a large number of employees in one location. For example, Jessica works for a big company that owns several nurseries, each with at least several hundred employees. She was the first person from the Alto Balsas to start working for them soon after she and her husband arrived in California, although many other workers from Mexico were already working there. Today five other women and three men from Jessica's hometown also work there; they all got their jobs based on her recommendations. However, workers in that company do not have nearly as much input into their hours or conditions of work as in the case of workers in the chain of donut shops, and it is more difficult, although not impossible, to get permission to take time off. Jessica gave me some insights into what this company expects of its workers:

> We are told that we have to concentrate on our work, and that we have to leave behind all our domestic problems and worries and think only about what we are doing. You have to work very fast, so the time also goes by quickly. Before you know it, the day is over. When we are grafting, we have to jot down what we have done. They don't check that each time, but once

the plants are taller, they will right away know if the numbers are correct; if you have underestimated, they will dock your pay.

Jessica's stories about her job illustrate how migrant workers are well aware of the importance of following the rules and getting along with the other workers in order to keep their jobs, as well as to conform to the already established reputation of Mexicans as good workers. They have no other choice but to be compliant and flexible, because their lack of legal status makes them very vulnerable. Jessica always carries water and soda pop for the person doing the grafting to ensure that person's cooperation. It is her job to follow behind with a bag of elastic bands, tying up each graft, but she needs to persuade the person doing the grafting to also help her by waiting at the end of each row until Jessica is finished making entries in her notepad. She told me that if the other worker were to proceed before she finished, she would fall behind, and the inserted grafts might fall off. Then they would have to start all over again in that section. However, not everyone is able to conform to the expectations of their employer. A man from Jessica's hometown was dismissed for being a slacker and for bringing in liquor to the workplace.

Jessica does not complain about her pay, nor does she ever grumble about her work the way that American-born workers who have higher expectations might, especially if they once had steady jobs with benefits. At the same time, she takes pride in her ability to do a variety of jobs in the nursery. Her job is more permanent than that of her husband, so she has become the family's main breadwinner. However, Jessica is also aware of, and stressed to me, the strict standards of her employer and their tight control over the workplace: "The company does not allow anyone to approach the workers. Not even my husband can visit me. They had told us that when we are working, planting trees or helping the grafters, that we have no friends, family, or spouse the way we do outside of work."

The relationship between Toribio and his boss, Mike, the owner of a much smaller business, took a more personal form. Mike is a millionaire who lives in a big house, and he once gave Toribio the keys to his house while he was away for a vacation. He showed Toribio his swimming pool and told him he could invite his friends over to have a party. Mike helped Toribio in other ways: "I bought my first car from Mike. He sold it to me for half of what is was worth. He also sold a good, inexpensive car to my

sister Paula when she came to live with me in California." Mike and Toribio have a good relationship bordering on friendship and they continue
to be on good terms, even when there is no work. This was not the case for
Baltazar, who did not regard a former boss very highly:

> In 1989 I started earning forty dollars a week in a textile mill when I was
> still inexperienced. Afterwards I got the knack of it and in 1990 I was earn-
> ing eighty dollars [far below the minimum wage, which was $3.80 an hour,
> or $152 a week, in 1990] and finally they put me on a salary of 180 dollars
> a week. That was raised to $190 in 1991. At that time I was ironing, sepa-
> rating the different clothes according to size and putting clothes into plastic
> bags. I did a bit of everything. My salary stayed the same for two years but I
> wanted another increase to $200. My boss told me that was not possible, that
> he had helped me and now it was time for me to help him. So I said I would
> prefer to do piecework and I started to earn on a piecework basis. By the end
> of the first week I had earned $270. That shows how my boss was sucking
> me dry before, that he was eating but not me.

Most of the textile factories in Los Angeles are owned by Koreans, most
of whom speak Spanish which they learned in Argentina, the country to
which they had first emigrated. They moved to the United States and set
up, or bought, textile factories as well as retail outlets in the fashion district
because it was the best option for investing their money. However, few of
them had any prior experience in the textile industry. Each owner in this
highly competitive industry has his or her own style of management, which
their undocumented workers consider to be inflexible. However, the owners of some of the smaller firms know how to treat their workers well and
gain their trust, as in the case of Joo-won, a Korean boss who adopted the
Spanish name Nicanor when he was in Argentina. Nicanor is highly regarded for being fair and patient. One of his former employees, Feliciano,
who arranged for me to visit the factory where he used to work, told me:

> Nicanor started running this textile factory several years ago. He speaks
> good Spanish and even learned a few words of Nahuatl. Nicanor prefers
> to hire undocumented workers from my hometown because he knows that
> we are good workers and willing to work extra hours when necessary. He
> knows that we will not just work for a short time and then leave. One day
> Nicanor jokingly told me that he had so many workers from my hometown
> that he should register his business with a Nahuatl name.

Although Feliciano liked, and got along with, his boss, he was also aware that Nicanor is also working outside of the law. Feliciano did not hesitate to go and work in another textile factory when he saw a better opportunity there, yet he keeps on good terms with Nicanor, who still employs other workers from Feliciano's hometown. He was also very aware that his former employer is vulnerable: "Nicanor does not have proper insurance and he gets nervous when inspectors come around to check working conditions. He will either shut down his operation or get us to lie to the inspector about how many hours we work there. By law we are only supposed to work eight hours a day, but sometimes we work eleven hours." Nicanor, the Korean boss with the Spanish name, is very informal and asks his workers to address him on a first-name basis. Feliciano is also very aware of how Nicanor tries to gain his workers' sympathy and understanding:

> One day, when we were fooling around, the boss proposed that we have a contest to see who is the fattest. He thought that Omar was the fattest and that I was fourth, and then he told me, "You should have seen me before; I was even fatter than Omar." Nicanor then said, "Do you know how you can lose a lot of weight really quickly? Get yourself a textile factory." He told me being the boss was very stressful because he was always worrying about the business, how his competitors might take away some of his orders, how his workers were always complaining about how little they earned, and how he never knew whether or not be would be able to survive.

As I spoke more about the textile industry with Feliciano and other undocumented Nahua workers in Los Angeles, I realized that they are quite aware of the nature of the textile industry and their place in it. They know that the Koreans are organized into family enterprises, each with their own internal hierarchies. Some Koreans specialize in cutting fabric using large mold presses before the individual pieces are shipped out to the textile factories to be sewn together and then distributed to both retail and wholesale outlets owned by related family cartels. Feliciano knows that Nicanor was being trained to run a textile factory even though he did not know much about the textile industry when he was first appointed as owner. He also told me that his former boss learned most of what he knew by hiring Rodolfo, a young man from Feliciano's hometown, as his main manager. Rodolfo, who is also undocumented, had figured out what was needed to ensure that a textile factory ran smoothly. He knew that it was important to first calculate the cost of making each piece; that the various stages of production have to be well coordinated; and that is was essential not to order too much cloth. It soon became obvious that Nicanor was initially just as dependent on Rodolfo and other undocumented workers as they were dependent on him. But while the case of Nicanor represents an almost symbiotic, but at the same time paternalistic, relationship between owner and migrant workers, those workers will not hesitate to lodge grievances if they feel an employer has overstepped the bounds, as we saw in the last chapter. Unfortunately, such grievance might not go anywhere, especially in the textile industry. As one worker explained to me:

> Factory owners are more likely to take advantage of their workers in December, which is a real slack period. One owner I know promised to pay the wages he owed by issuing a check but told us that we would need to wait for a while. But instead of paying what he owed for wages by the date he had promised, he simply shut down the factory. We later learned that he opened a new factory in another location several months later. We could have lodged a grievance but knew we would not get anything because that is very difficult; the owner had not registered his business and the government did not know his real name.

The fact that Rodolfo, an undocumented worker, became a manager in another factory shows that lack of a work permit does not prevent some workers from getting ahead, especially in an economic sector that is itself largely unregulated and conducted illegally. However, being an undocumented manager had its own drawbacks, as I found by talking to Rodolfo during my second visit to Los Angeles. I was also interested in finding out more about his background, how he had become the manager and how long that job lasted:

> I did not do any work in our family corn plot in Mexico nor did I have to take care of animals. My father gave me permission to attend school full time and study hard. After finishing school I helped an uncle to sell crafts to tourists in Rincon de Huayabitos. That is where I learned a smattering of English but I still have difficulty speaking it although I have been in the U.S. for eleven years. I first got to know Nicanor when he was working as a manager for a warehouse for clothing. At that time I worked in a textile factory in L.A. Nicanor wanted to set up his own factory and told me he

had already bought seven sewing machines and rented the space he needed to set up his own business. When he told me one day that he wanted me to be his manager, I thought he was joking. That is how I became the person in charge of the day-to-day operations, including finding workers. At first only one worker was from my hometown. He knew how to operate one of the more complicated machines. The rest were Guatemalans and workers from other parts of Mexico. However, I gradually found more people from my hometown, whom I knew already had experience. The factory expanded and we ended up with twenty machines. I was his manager for only two and a half years and quit that job because it was too stressful. I had a lot of responsibility and also put in long hours. I am now working in a clothing warehouse where I do packing, organize merchandise, and also some sales. I prefer that work, even though I now earn less money.

On my second trip to Los Angeles I met another undocumented worker from Rodolfo's hometown who was also a manager in a textile factory, this time for four years. His story is somewhat different. Antonio's father, a guitarist, also believed in the importance of education. His paternal grandfather, who became a successful craft vendor, served as his role model. Antonio planned to accomplish something in life, including forming his own band in the United States. He achieved this goal within five years of his arrival of the United States when his band, Vuelo Norteño, produced its own CD. His work career, in which he started as a textile worker, can be used to illustrate the ambition, entrepreneurship, and hard work that characterize many migrant workers from Mexico. Yet his inability to pursue his dream of setting up his own business illustrates the roadblocks that stand in the way of undocumented workers who could have gone much further if they had the same opportunities available to legal immigrants. I met Antonio in a restaurant, where he insisted on paying the bill.

A lot of other textile workers prefer to work on the same machine, whichever one allows them to earn more money doing piecework. They do not want to take on other jobs that would help them get ahead in the long run. But I am always looking for new challenges to better myself. I started at the bottom, was ironing after a month, and a year later I started using a sewing machine. I learned how to sew on one of the easier machines in just one week, but I wanted to learn how to use every machine they had so that I would eventually be able to work as a manager. Whenever I was good enough on one machine I would do piecework for a while, but then ask for a different machine, for a more complicated task, and go back on a lower weekly salary of four hundred dollars a week. I noticed that the American-born managers with college diplomas did not have any practical experience, that they had never worked in a textile factory. Most of those managers did not last long. So I persuaded my boss, who was also the owner, to make me his manager. He agreed. I did that from 2007 until 2011 when he was bought out by a larger company, also owned by Koreans. They kept me on but asked me to work in a different operation they owned, also in L.A., where I learned how to create samples for the workers in their textile divisions.

When I asked Antonio how he learned his new job, using photos to make clothing samples using paper sheets, he told me he was allowed to take courses in a special training school. He attended classes for three hours in the afternoons and on Saturdays while he continued working for the new company. He had to pay for attending those classes, but stopped taking formal classes after three months when he felt he had learned enough to do the job. However, he did not take formal classes long enough to be able to make designs on the computer. Antonio pointed out that even full-time students would have to study for two or three years in order to obtain a diploma, but that would cost them fifteen thousand dollars. However, he was not interested in getting a diploma and continued to learn on the job. Today, Antonio is happy in his new job, which does not involve a lot of stress, and he earns almost the same salary as when he was a manager overseeing fifty workers. I also asked Antonio whether he was planning to start his own business to advance further in his career. His answer was that it would be absolutely impossible, since he is an undocumented worker without any chance of becoming legalized. As someone without legal status, he would not be able to register any enterprise he set up in his own name. He considered owning an unregistered business as too risky since he would be deported if he were caught. His only way of being his own boss to some extent is to sell products for Amway, as we saw in chapter 6, but he did not really consider that as having his own business.

Undocumented workers like Antonio or Rodolfo do have some room to maneuver if their skills and experience are in demand. In other cases, such as that of Evangelina, who works in a donut shop, undocumented workers can negotiate time off work by offering to find replacements. However, even though undocumented workers may sometimes have a say in who gets hired, overall they are at a disadvantage. They are still vulnerable and more likely to be cheated. In all cases, undocumented workers would have been much better off if they were legal in the eyes of the law. We have seen how some American employers treat their undocumented workers fairly, and even go out their way to help, but this is often not the case. For every success story there are stories of employers laying off workers without notice so that they can hire others willing to work for even lower wages.

Maximina and her husband were among the few people from the Alto Balsas who left to seek a better life in the United States in the early eighties. However, they went back and forth too many times to benefit from the legalization program that was under way during their third stay. Nevertheless, Maximina did obtain a valid Social Security number. Several years later, her employer asked her to provide a different Social Security number each year, without giving her a reason, so she assumed that her boss's request was just an excuse to lay her off. This action caused considerable distress because Sergio, her husband, had also just lost his job. Maximina and her husband are exceptions because they had bought a house. They had set up a bank account and kept all of their income tax receipts to get approval for a mortgage, and in 1992 this migrant couple became the proud owners of an old bungalow. They fixed it up and sold it several years later. At that time Sergio had been working for a rental company for ten years. This couple then used the $9,000 equity they had thus far accumulated to buy a bigger house. However, they could no longer keep up with their monthly payments when neither of them had a job. They lost all of their investments, including a new truck, and are now back living in rented quarters.

The setback experienced by another undocumented couple with six children was somewhat different. We have already met them. Juan worked for a large landscaping firm for six years, starting at $7.50 an hour. Every year he got a raise until he was earning close to twenty dollars an hour. Then, suddenly, in 2000, he and five workers were let go. Two months later Juan started working for another, smaller company for $12.50 an hour. However, this was not a full-time job. He was called in to work only two days a week, and often had to work at distant locations two hours' drive from where he lives. Nevertheless, Juan was able to stay in their rented townhouse because his wife, Jessica, whom we have already met several time, started working six days a week in a plant nursery. She started working there part-time after the birth of her fourth child, but her children were then old enough for her to take on a full-time job.

The situation of millions of Mexican migrants is insecure and there is little they can do about it. Undocumented workers who work for wages do not like the fact that they are not paid for overtime or get vacation pay, but they do not want to jeopardize their jobs by reporting this to the authorities. They have accepted this as part of the job. Nevertheless, although they have few legal protections and little room to negotiate with their employers, undocumented workers will not hesitate to quit a job if someone else offers more pay and better working conditions. We have already seen how Toribio, who first worked in Texas, moved to California to take a job where he could earn more money. Undocumented workers want to earn as much as possible to meet all their needs, send remittances back home and have some money left over. It is not surprising that most of them work so hard. They work long hours, and do so without complaining, to cover what they consider to be their basic needs plus a bit more. Undocumented migrants from Mexico have to work especially hard in order to keep up their group reputation as ideal employees.

"We Can Never Hang Out with Our Friends"

As more people from the Alto Balsas started living in the United States, household and family dynamics in both the United States and their home region were transformed, including patterns of courtship and how children are raised. This chapter focuses on the children of migrants, including those who are American citizens by virtue of their birth in the United States. Most of them have spent all or most of their lives in the United States and would not know what it is like to live in the towns in Mexico where their parents and grandfathers grew up. Others, who were raised in Mexico, have fond memories of growing up in their hometowns in Guerrero. I have interacted with some whom I knew both in Mexico and after they came to the United States.

Initially, only a few married women crossed the border to join their husbands already living in the United States, taking their children with them. This was the case for the woman from whom I rented a room in Mexico in 2003; she left to join her husband a year later. Her two young children, one of whom was about to start kindergarten, subsequently had all their schooling in the United States. In other cases, older children who were already attending primary school were subsequently enrolled in American schools, which could be difficult at first. One young man who had barely finished third grade in Mexico told me:

> I could not understand my teacher because she only spoke English, and the other kids from Mexico poked fun at me because I did not even speak very good Spanish. I almost quit but my parents told me to try harder. I finally learned to speak good Spanish from the friends I made at school, but I did not really learn English until I was in middle school. I did not start getting good marks until I started high school.

Other indigenous undocumented children, who mastered Spanish before arriving in the United States, learned English within two or three years, which made them trilingual. In contrast, their parents, who for the most part operate in a Spanish-speaking American work environment, are still struggling with their English or have never learned it. As more children of undocumented workers were born in the United States, a whole generation of young Nahuas automatically became American citizens. Very few of these American-born children speak Nahuatl; most of them at least understand what their parents are saying but they often answer in English. Such American-born children have no trouble understanding Spanish, although they do not write it.

In Nahua communities, relations between parents and children and between younger and older people in general were very formal prior to around 1960. Children were not supposed to talk back to adults and had to show respect to their elders. Even a grown man, already married, would kiss his father's hand. An unmarried man was expected to ask his father's permission as well as advice before making any important financial decisions. I still observed some remnants of that in the twenty-first century. A bachelor in Cuernavaca, the art vendor we met earlier, still feels the need to consult his father whenever he goes traveling and to get approval for many decisions. He told me he even had to make sure that his father was in favor of agreeing to be interviewed. When I was attending a family party in Guerrero, I was surprised when a teacher asked me to invite his elderly father to have another glass of tequila during a party held in his house. The teacher was the host, but he told me it did not feel right for him to offer his father a drink.

Following the introduction of public education, the social distance and power differential between now literate children and their illiterate parents in Mexico diminished. Young educated men assumed public posts previously reserved for their elders, and adults who had not gone to school became dependent on younger children to read documents written in Spanish. Since most older adults were not fully conversant in Spanish they depended on their now completely bilingual older children to explain what exactly a government official or traveling salesmen was trying to tell them. This dependence on children to do translation was replicated in the United States where parents who learned how to read and write Spanish in Mexican schools would not be able to read or write anything written in English. Older children acted as translators between their parents and landlords, teachers, neighbors, or storeowners who do not speak Spanish.

It is not easy to bring up children in the United States when both parents have to work. It costs more to buy clothes and food and children growing up in large urban centers have higher expectations than their counterparts in Mexico. Children want to have the latest video games to play on TV consoles at home and wear the same trendy clothes as their American schoolmates. The network of relatives, especially grandparents and older aunts and uncles available for babysitting or supervising children, is smaller than it was in Mexico. This is true even in places where a concentration of migrants from the same hometowns ensures close-knit communities. Parents do their best. I know of several undocumented couples who have taken on cousins or siblings as boarders, who in return for room and board help out with cooking and watch over their kids. Groups of parents take turns dropping off their kids at each other's houses. Older children look after younger siblings if their parents have not yet arrived by the time they come home from school. However, this support system can occasionally break down, as I witnessed when I spent ten days living with one couple.

Both Eugenio and Teresa have steady jobs, although their schedules overlap to some degree. Her daily routine consists of getting up at 4:30 A.M. to make sandwiches for her kids, before driving off to start a shift that begins at 6 A.M. Her husband usually cleans up in the kitchen, and gets the kids to school on time before he drives to his job. However, one day he too had to leave early to go to work, taking his oldest son with him. When I came out of my room and entered the kitchen that morning I saw one of the younger children use a chair to climb on top of the kitchen counter, to reach a cupboard for a box of instant soup. Another child put a pot of water on the stove, which almost spilled when the water started boiling. Luckily there was no accident. I later found out that a neighbor who had promised to drop by early had not shown up.

Unlike their grandparents' generation, younger undocumented workers believe in the importance of education. The American teachers I have met told me they find the parents of the Mexican students they teach to be supportive and willing to come to meetings. Parents who have cars drive their children to school and they insist that their children do their homework, even though they cannot be of much assistance because of their limited knowledge of English. California has schools with bilingual English-Spanish programs with Spanish-speaking teachers, in which the majority of students are Latinos. Such schools not only help ease the transition for children with limited exposure to English but allow their parents from the Alto Balsas, who usually speak Spanish as well as Nahuatl, to better communicate with teachers.

Parents who are undocumented are quite aware of the difference in the quality in education among different schools. I came across at least one case where a family even moved to another neighborhood that had a school with better teachers, even though one parent had to travel farther to go to work. However, not all parents have a preference for bilingual schools. Some of them think that it is better for their children to attend schools where they hear only English from both teachers and other students on the playground. In general, I found that migrants in the United States took more interest in their children's education than parents in Mexico, where some part-time farmers or vendors did not give their children enough time to do their homework. Parents living in Mexico, especially those who did not receive much schooling, expect children to help out by working in the fields, fetching water, or helping out in the craft industry. Such parents do not really care whether their children pursue their studies beyond grade school or high school, although they will not try to dissuade them from going off to the United States. They hope that any children who migrate will earn money and send back remittances. On the other hand, Mexican parents who have themselves completed grade school are better able to help their children with their homework, because they can read Spanish even if they continue to speak Nahuatl at home.

Regardless of the attitudes of these parents toward education, students in Mexico walk back and forth to school and frequently visit relatives and friends. They go out on their own, or with other children, to fetch animals grazing in fields outside of the village town boundaries. Although parents in Mexico might be more demanding in terms of their expectations that their children do chores, they do not need to restrict their physical movement since the small towns on their home region do not present any dangers apart from the possibility of being bitten by a scorpion, which does not happen very often. In stark contrast, parents living in the United States do not allow their children to leave the house after coming home from school.

When I asked Ana, then fourteen years old, if she and her brother ever went out to hang out with their friends in Los Angeles, she said, "No—our parents don't allow that, nor can our friends come in and visit us here. We are stuck at home." That was the case for every family I knew. With the high rate of street crime and gangs in American cities, especially in places like downtown Los Angeles, parents are worried about their children either being the target of gang members or themselves getting involved in criminal activities. Parents are particularly worried about the possibility of teenage children getting in trouble with the law and being deported if those children are undocumented, a fear that it not unfounded as we will learn in the next chapter. This is yet another reason they want to keep close to home, especially as they grow older. However, these same parents do not worry when those children visits their hometowns, even if they go on their own. Children born in the United States sometimes make such trips to Mexico to visit their grandparents and other relatives.

Pedrito, the fifteen-year-old American-born son of Juan and Jessica, flew to his hometown on his own to attend the big annual festival there in 2011. He had not seen his hometown since he was a small boy, when the whole family went back for visit. Pedrito had a great time and hopes to make another trip to Mexico. While in Mexico he slept in the houses of both his paternal and maternal grandparents and hung out with several cousins. In the fall of 2012, a fourteen-year-old girl and her brother made a trip to visit their parents' hometown in Mexico where they stayed several weeks in their grandmother's house. There were no feasts or parties during their stay, but they made the rounds of the houses of several aunts and uncles, including the family with whom I ended up staying several months later. That aunt later reported to me the conversations she had had with that girl:

> When my niece and nephew came to visit me, I asked them what they thought of our town. My niece, who is older than her brother, and better able to express herself, told me that life here is not as hectic as in the U.S. She liked the freedom she had to leave the house where she was staying. She told me that her life in Mexico was completely different than in the U.S. where they have to stay indoors all the time.

Parents in the United States know that their children will be staying up late for village festivals when they go to Mexico, and that they might not get back to the houses where they are staying until late at night. But they know they will be safe. Robert Courtney Smith, who spent fifteen years doing research on Mexicans in New York, noticed a similar contrast between how even older children are practically confined to the apartments or townhouses where they live in the United States compared with the freedom they have in Mexico. He gives as an example a teenage girl born in the United States whose parents gave her permission to travel on her own to attend a village festival in their hometown in the state of Puebla; but these same parents had a strict rule about her coming straight home to their apartment in Brooklyn after school, where their daughter had to wait for her parents to come home.

In my study I wanted to include young people who had jobs, but whose parents had brought them to the United States when they were not yet ready to enter the workforce. Delfino, the young man in the van mentioned in the preface, was eight years old when his family crossed the border. When I first met him in Mexico during one of his return visits he was already a teenager living with the retired teacher in the United States. That teacher later recounted how he ended up living in her house.

> When Delfino came here he had a hard time adapting. Both his eardrums were pierced, so he had a hard time hearing and had real problems at school. He was also very skinny and undernourished. They put him in a Spanish school but he did not even speak Spanish and got terribly behind and would lose his temper. At that time Delfino's mother was working for us, cooking and cleaning. She asked me if I would be willing to let Delfino live with me so I could help him with his studying. I talked it over with my oldest

daughter who was then living with me, and we decided to give it a try. I attended a meeting with Delfino's parents and three school principals, telling them I wanted Delfino to move in with us that same day so he could adapt as quickly as possible. It was difficult for him at first because he was not used to following a schedule.

With the teacher's help, Delfino got the proper medical attention he had not received (that is how his hearing problem was diagnosed) and he learned to speak fluent English. However, she was not as successful in helping him become legalized. The problem is that Delfino had gone back and forth to Mexico too often as he was growing up, and was caught twice. While attending high school, Delfino met a young woman from his hometown whose parents are also undocumented workers. He got her pregnant so Delfino had to start earning money to pay for the expenses of raising a child. I paid them a visit in 2011, and ordered a meal in the restaurant where he was working as a busboy. The next time I paid a visit to Delfino, in February 2012, he was working as a waiter in an upscale restaurant. The baby was doing well but the young couple was still living in a room in the teacher's house.

The transition from being a young man, undocumented but studying in the United States, to someone who has to work to support a family is not easy. Delfino told me about his older brother who got married several years earlier:

> It was really tough for my brother when he got married because he had always lived with other people who took care of him, especially my mother. He got married at the age of nineteen, but he and his wife continued to live at my sister's house. When they told my brother that he was going to become responsible for paying the bills, something he had never done, and when he realized he was not earning enough money, he cried. He started working for GBS, a drug store, and later worked for Walgreen's. He now has to work every day.

Unlike most of their parents, the young people who came to the United States as teenagers will have completed six years of elementary education, which means they are at least literate in Spanish. They may even have a chance to learn English through further schooling, which enables them to get better jobs. Raul, who was only fourteen when he became an undocumented worker, told me: "I started working for a Taco Bell right away, serving people, but I had a hard time because I did not know any English. So I went to high school here for one year, which helped me a lot. I now work as a cashier for Burger King, and no longer in the kitchen like so many of the kids who only went to grade school in Mexico." Once they start working and earning money, the undocumented children of undocumented parents may still be living at home. But if they are still single it is expected that they will obey their parents, which can lead to tensions and misunderstandings.

Leonardo, Juan and Jessica's oldest son, was still living at home at age eighteen and doing some part-time work. He spent a lot of time at home playing video games and spent most of the money he earned paying the fifty dollars a month for a Wi-Fi connection so that he can download the most recent programs. His mother asks him to help out by driving his younger sisters to school events and doing some cleaning around the house. She gets very angry when he drinks too much, especially when that means he cannot take the car to run errands and she has to do it instead. In 2012, while attending a family gathering, I overheard Jessica talking about Leonardo to another woman who is a good friend of Juan and Jessica: "My son tells me he does not want me to boss him around anymore, to tell him what to do. So I said to him, 'I am the one who has to earn the money to keep the household running—that as long as I am supporting you, I am going to give the orders.'" Two years later, when Leonardo was still living at home, he played a major role in his sister's *quinceañera*, as one of the seven *chambelanes* or young men that accompany the girl celebrating her fifteenth-year birthday party. He also organized the party bus that took them to an outing to a restaurant and an amusement park after attending a mass. Jessica is glad that her son is turning out to be a responsible young man, given that he went through a difficult period as a teenager. He had once been picked up by the police for a minor misdemeanor and put on probation. If Leonardo had gotten into more serious problems with the law, he could technically have been deported, since he was born in Mexico. Leonardo and Delfino have both turned out alright, but other young men from the Alto Balsas region who came to the United States as children were not as lucky, as we shall see in the next chapter.

10

"They Only Send You Back if You Are Bad"

I heard about Cristino, Delfino's cousin, during one of my stays in Houston, but I met him for the first time in Mexico. He had recently been deported for drinking while driving. In the United States, Cristino had worked in a supermarket and had paid off his coyote. Back in his hometown he was working as a bricklayer's assistant. I saw him using a hand shovel to mix cement and gravel. He told me he did not like what he was doing and disliked his wages even more; he earned less per week than what he earned in a couple of hours in the United States. His situation shows that undocumented workers pay a heavy price for the mistakes they make.

Illegal migrants may come into contact with law enforcement agents for a variety of reasons. They might be stopped for speeding, or be approached by a policeman who is checking up on a noisy party. However, police are usually not interested in someone's immigration status, only whether or not someone is breaking the law when it comes to driving, property crimes, or drug possession. One day, when Delfino was driving me around, he told me about his first encounter with American policemen. As we passed a schoolyard, he said:

> I have vivid memories of this place because we used to take over this little park. People brought their children and played here while the young men played basketball [He pointed to a fenced-off cement court with three sets of basketball hoops]. There were two gates that used to be open and we would just go in. We liked the big *cancha* [outdoor basketball court] and the way it was enclosed with a fence, but we were not supposed to play here. The police would come by and tell us to leave. The school started to lock the gates but we would just climb over the fence. I do not think they minded because we only came here late afternoons and in the evening. We even brought our own battery-powered spotlights. So the police would come again but they saw that we did no harm. They used to laugh and thought we were crazy to play so late at night. One of them said, "You guys must really like basketball."

The undocumented workers I know all have a high regard for the police. They compare the professional conduct of U.S. police with the corruption and incompetence of Mexican police from the time they used to live there. I did not hear any complaints about police harassment. To the contrary, one undocumented woman thought the police in the United States could be quite helpful; a policewoman had helped her recover a car that was stolen.

Undocumented migrants are familiar with other kinds of American security personnel. In one town in California undocumented workers organized dances to raise money for their hometown as well as to celebrate weddings and baptisms. These are family events, with people of various ages, including children. They always serve alcohol, so the organizers would sometimes ask for security in case fights broke out, or if any strangers tried to crash the party. Organizers pay $250 for three guards who stay for several hours. I have attended several such parties. In 2013 I noticed how security guards, who had mainly kept to the sidelines, approached two men who were getting argumentative during a dance organized to celebrate a baptism held earlier that day. However, just as they were ready to escort a drunk man ready to pick a fight, his wife, as well as several of his friends, intervened by breaking the two apart and telling the security guards that they had the situation under control. As people were leaving at the end of the evening, several designated drivers drove home those who had drunk too much. I was later told that if the city police suspected that a migrant who was tipsy might be driving home late at night after such an event, they would turn a blind eye. I suspect that the person who told me this was probably exaggerating or unrealistic in his expectation that the city policy would look the other way if they suspected someone of drinking and driving. Yet his comments certainly indicate that city police are seen as lenient, as they are in other matters, such as driving without a license, as we shall see later.

The gap between the leniency of city police and the punitive actions of officials from Immigration and Customs Enforcement (ICE) is narrowing. Federal agents would like the police to report the whereabouts of illegal migrants, and the state of Arizona has passed a law requiring the police to do so. Yet despite ever stricter laws designed to make their lives less comfortable, people kept telling me they are not worried about getting in trouble with the law. The most common statement heard over and over again, at least up to as late as 2012, is, "If you work hard and don't commit any crimes, you will not get arrested." However, undocumented workers cannot get away from their illegal status. During my last visit, in 2013, I became aware that the situation of undocumented workers has become very fluid and that even people who have been in the United States for some time are getting leery.

Paula, whom we met earlier, was not worried that she might be deported when I spoke to her in 2012. Today, at least on the surface, she seems to lead a normal life; but she is painfully aware that under a new, stricter policy, she will no longer be able to use her now expired Mexican driver's license in the American state were she now lives and works. Paula is very aware of the limitations of her lack of legal status and wonders what will happen in the future if she were ever stopped by the police. Undocumented workers who cannot apply for, or renew, driver's licenses, as is the case in most American states, are in a quandary. They need to drive to get to work but do not know what they will do if they are ever stopped. Their employers do not like this situation but can do little to help out, and city police who do not like the new regulation are faced with a difficult choice when they have to issue a ticket. Juan faced this dilemma when he was stopped for speeding:

> Last year I got a ticket going over the speed limit when I was exiting a ramp on the freeway. There were two policemen on motorcycles. That speeding

ticket cost me four hundred dollars and I am still paying it off. When one of the policemen asked for my driver's license, I told him I did not have one. He told me I would not be able to drive for one year and that someone else would have to come to pick up my car. I phoned my boss and asked him to come and get me, but when he arrived the policemen had already gone. I just got back in my car and went on my way.

Juan has to be more careful in the future and may yet be able to apply for a driver's license in California under a new law. But he cannot afford to make any more mistakes:

Nowadays the police are very strict. They will lock you up and then deport you. That never happened before. Before, if a police officer caught you drinking and driving, they would give you a ticket and you had to go to a special school that deals with problems of alcoholism. You had to do community service and also pay a fine. The second time you would have to pay even more but they would deport you only after the third time.

Undocumented workers do not think it is fair that the American government will not give them work permits; however, they appreciate the fairness of other parts of the American legal system. This is the case even when they run into problems with the law. One former migrant told me: "In the U.S. they apply the law, unlike Mexico where one can pay a bribe to get released or to stay out of jail. I like the American system. When you get fined, you can either pay with money or with labor." Most undocumented workers think it is a good idea that people who commit serious crimes serve time in jail. They think judges are too lenient.

During the Obama administration more undocumented Mexicans, including juvenile delinquents, were deported than under any previous administration. In the Alto Balsas, starting in 2012, such deported delinquents started showing up in several towns. They are called *cholos*; the clothes they wear and their tattoos do not conform to local norms. They don't work, shout obscenities, and are suspected of breaking into empty houses. The attitudes and behavior of these young people engendered fear and hostility in their home communities. Some of these fears are unfounded. Virginia, a local teacher, told me about one of her nephews, who had spent some time in an American jail: "I felt pity, especially when I saw tattoos all over his body. He was pressured into getting those tattoos. But he said to me, '*Tia* [aunt], don't feel sorry for me. What happened to me is my own stupid fault. I am still paying for my mistakes.'"

Unfortunately, some of those who get deported are hard-core delinquents who belonged to street gangs in the United States. In Mexico I heard complaints about how some of them were letting the air out of tires and stealing rims. I was told that those *cholos* learn bad habits in the United States and how they get angry and blame the *comisario municipal* (village mayor, who also acts as judge) when they have to spend a couple of hours in the village jail. People who live in Nahua towns cannot understand why these miscreants will not accept the fact that they are being punished for doing something that is wrong. People in both Mexico and the United States were scandalized when some *cholos* went over the line. Gaudencio, who has been the United States for a long time, but who keeps up with what is happening in his hometown, told me about what happened:

> The village authorities are scared of these delinquents. When my uncle Niceforo was *comisario suplente* [deputy mayor] he ordered several of them to be locked up in the town jail. When they were released, they attacked my uncle and hit him, they almost killed him. My uncle was driving in his truck in front of the church when they made him stop and beat him up.

The initial problem with some of these former gang members who were deported got worse, as shown by a rash of roadside robberies on the outskirts of a town in the Alto Balsas that had not seen this kind of crime since the time of the Mexican Revolution. For several months no one knew who the perpetrators were, until the police caught a seventeen year old who had previously been in trouble with the law in California. Back in Mexico, he became the ringleader of a group of boys, aged twelve to eighteen. Not only did the leader plan all the robberies, but during the last robbery he shot the driver of a small truck, a young man struggling to set up a business selling drinking water. The wounded driver died in the hospital, leaving a wife and two small children. This crime is a clear indication that there is a basis to the fear of parents about the corrupting influence of big American cities.

With the perpetrators of these crimes now locked up in a Mexican jail, people in the Alto Balsas had less reason to worry about more armed robberies in what had up until now been a peaceful region. However, an increase in kidnappings and assaults in the rest of Guerrero and other

Mexican states is likely to result in more people from the Alto Balsas attempting to cross the border. Local craft vendors, who still travel to other parts of Mexico, are facing greater dangers; in 2011, one of them was robbed at gunpoint by men who confiscated his pickup truck and forced him to walk to the nearest town in the state of Toluca. The U.S.-Mexico border region in particular is known for its high crime going back at least twenty years. In 2002, the last time Juan was on his way back to California, he was robbed and beaten in the border town of Tijuana. However, up until the recent robberies in one town in the Alto Balsas, undocumented worker still thought their home region was safe.

We have seen earlier how some people left their younger children in the care of grandparents in Mexico, because they were worried about their children growing up to become delinquents. Others, who would not dream of leaving their children behind when they are small, thought it would be a good idea to send their older, school-age children born in the United States back to Mexico. Alberto and Santa, who were already married when they moved to Los Angeles, both ended up working there. Their oldest son was born in their hometown and they had two more boys in the United States. One of their American-born children, Apolinar, became a juvenile delinquent and already had a record at age sixteen, when his parents sent him to Mexico to go and live with Alberto's parents. The boy had been there only once, in 1995, when the whole family went back for a short visit. The idea was that it was more likely he would be reformed if he were to spend a couple of years in the supportive environment of a small town in Mexico. They figured Apolinar would enjoy the fresh air and learn how to work. However, he was bored, could not smoke, and missed his friends in Los Angeles. He gave his grandparents a hard time and Alberto's parents finally gave up and begged their son to have Apolinar sent back to Los Angeles; he is now back in the United States. I do not know what happened to Fortunato, an eight-year-old boy whom I met in Mexico several years ago. His parents sent him back to Mexico after he was expelled from school. Fortunato was surprised to hear me speaking Nahuatl in his uncle's village store and told me, "I do not know that language you are speaking." He looked lost and bewildered. I still wonder what will happen to him and what he will do when he grows up.

Juan and Jessica wanted to make arrangements for their American-born son, Pedrito, to spend a year or two in Mexico. His older brother, who had already made a short trip to Mexico to attend the annual festival in his hometown, was mentioned in the last chapter. He likes his hometown; however, Pedrito's parents changed their minds when they realized that their hometown might not be as safe as they thought, as Jessica told me:

> I would have liked for Pedrito to learn how to work in the *milpa* [cornfield], just as I was taught when I was his age. But we are afraid to send him because of all the kidnappings and assaults that are taking place in Mexico. Now there are even problems in my hometown. One of my nephews there, Benjamin, joined up with the *cholos* who got into trouble in both Mexico and the U.S.A. It is no longer safe there. A friend of mine also wanted to send her children back to San Juan Tetelcingo but she is not going to do that now.

It turns out that I knew the nephew to whom she was referring when he was still attending the village high school in Mexico. I remember Benjamin as a handsome young man who performed dances portraying native warriors at school events, and as the best hunter in his hometown. He used to go out at night with an old rifle and always managed to come home with some small game to supplement the family's meager meals. He was popular with the girls and seemed self-confident. During a stay in Mexico in 2008 I heard that he had gone off to the United States with a girlfriend from a Spanish-speaking town. Three years later, when I was in California, someone told me that Benjamin had been locked up in an American jail. I did not hear the story of what happened until the following year.

> One of Benjamin's older brothers is a member of a street gang in the U.S. He knows that his younger brother has a good aim with a rifle and so, soon after Benjamin arrived in Los Angeles, he invited him to join a street gang. There was a shoot-out in which a much younger black boy was killed. Benjamin was blamed for the boy's death, even though he did not pull the trigger that killed him. He was put in jail and is still awaiting a court case. His girlfriend has broken up with him.

I was not able to find out exactly what happened, since I heard various confusing, third-hand accounts of the events that led to Benjamin's arrest. Apparently he was transferred to another jail, in Sacramento, and someone speculated that after another couple of months in that jail Benjamin would probably be deported to Mexico. Other people though he would stay in jail for a long time, and might even die there. I later found out that Benjamin's older brother, who was also summoned for questioning, has since fled and is hiding somewhere in Chicago.

Who knows what will happen to Benjamin. He might end up being deported and end up living with his mother again, but he will have a hard time readapting to life in Mexico, just like many other teenagers and young men who have been deported (I have so far not heard of any women who have been deported). Most have spent enough time in the United States to have learned passable English and claim they can no longer speak or understand Nahuatl. They will probably end up leaving the Alto Balsas to live in Mexico City or some other Mexican urban center, as in the case of an eighteen-year-old man I met in Mexico soon after he was deported; Zacarias had already started living with, and then left, a woman in the United States. He told me he was planning to go and live with his sister who sells crafts in Cancun. But there is no guarantee that the young people who have been deported for misbehavior will not end up back in the United States. Cristino, whom we met at the beginning of this chapter, signed a letter promising that he would not go back to the United States for five years. One year later, in 2011, when I went to visit his cousin Delfino in Houston, he was back in Houston.

11

"We Must Carry On Our Ancestors' Traditions"

The stories so far presented are identical to those that could be told by undocumented workers from anywhere in Mexico. However, in some respects the experiences of migrants from the Alto Balsas are different from those of other Mexicans because they speak a language other than Spanish, and because they maintain the customs of indigenous communities. The way their remittances are spent is also different. In this regard my study more accurately represents the 20 percent of the Mexican population designated as *indígenas*, including 5 percent of Mexicans who identify as *indígenas* even though they no longer speak an indigenous language. The fact that there are indigenous as opposed to mestizo Mexicans was not reflected in American census data until the year 2000 with the inclusion on the category "Hispanic American Indians." Yet most Americans of Mexican descent are not aware that there are millions of people in Mexico who still speak a language other than Spanish as their mother tongue.

This fact first struck me when I flew into Sacramento in 2011. I was sitting beside a young woman whose parents had come to the United States as undocumented workers from one of Mexico's northern states. She spoke fluent English and Spanish, but was surprised when I told her that there are Mexicans who still speak Nahuatl and other indigenous languages. When I returned to Sacramento a year later, Albino, a young man proud of his ability to speak Nahuatl, told me about meeting Mexicans in the United States who were also not aware that there are *indígenas*:

> Someone I know told his children that all the people who speak Nahuatl had been killed a long time ago. So I introduced him to people right here who speak Nahuatl. Someone else, who was born in Mexico, knows that there are *indígenas* but he thinks that they live very far away in Mexico. I also had to prove to him that there are *indígenas* right here in Sacramento.

Migrants from the towns in the Alto Balsas regularly use Nahuatl at home, as well as when they speak to their relatives in Mexico on the phone. In contrast, the children of younger migrants generally understand, but do not speak, their parents' mother tongue. For example, the children of Alejandro, the man who wore a captain's uniform at his wedding, are fluent in both English and Spanish. Alex, his ten-year-old son who was born in the United States, told me:

> I do not know how to speak Nahuatl, although I can understand some of it. Like my brother and my sisters I speak Spanish at home. We all started learning English when we went to school. My parents used to speak Nahuatl with each other, but not to us. When I went to visit Mexico, my cousin spoke Nahuatl with her parents at home, but when she showed me around the village, she spoke to me in Spanish.

Many parents in the United States speak to their children using their mother tongue, but those children usually answer in Spanish. It is my impression that many of these children are not interested in, and might even be ashamed of, the language spoken by an older generation. In one of the households were I was staying, a sixteen-year old boy even poked fun at his mother when she was scolding him in Nahuatl. He imitated the way she was speaking. Those children may understand Nahuatl but are not likely to speak it very well; I actually had to teach one of those children some words in Nahuatl he did not understand.

Spanish is widely used in both the workplace and public settings in the United States, which adds yet another challenge for indigenous migrants who do not speak fluent Spanish. Ironically, older Nahua migrants who grew up in Guerrero at a time when most children did not attend school learned Spanish not in Mexico but in the United States! Carlos, now living in Mexico, told me:

> I worked in a garment factory in Los Angeles for eighteen years but did not learn a word of English. The other workers and the supervisors all spoke Spanish. In fact, I learned how to speak much better Spanish in the United States. The owner of the factory is Korean, and his wife sometimes tried to teach us Korean. So now I speak fluent Spanish, Mexicano, and even a bit of Korean, but still no English.

Carlos laments the fact that some of his hometown friends who sell handicrafts have at least picked up a few words of English through their contact with American tourists.

Nahua migrants feel more comfortable speaking Nahuatl than Spanish, but increasing mastery of Spanish through contact with other Mexicans is changing their social identities. Indigenous migrants who have spent a good part of their lives in the United States gradually develop a national identity as Spanish-speaking Mexicans. Their primary point of reference is no longer their hometown. We have seen how presenting themselves as Mexican in the United States, as opposed to some other group, can help them get jobs. In contrast, the children of undocumented workers who have grown up and gone to school in the United States see themselves primarily as Americans. These children are an integral part of a single, albeit ethnically diverse, American society. But they are also aware, or quickly learn, that they are not the same as other Mexican Americans. Not only do their parents and grandparents speak "that funny language," but they will have participated in ceremonies, festivals, and family rituals that are different from those of other children of Mexican descent. Moreover, they will have invariably heard a grandparent or an aunt talking about the importance of preserving the traditions of their ancestors.

We earlier encountered examples of a unique form of village governance and land ownership in Mexican indigenous communities. Anthropologists use the term "civil-religious hierarchy" or "cargo system." All male citizens of indigenous towns are expected to periodically assume public posts starting one year after they are married. Their wives help out by providing food for visitors or sweeping the village plaza. In such indigenous communities, religious duties and public service are closely intertwined, despite the strict separation between church and state in Mexico. In most of the villages of the Alto Balsas the head of a household living in the United States is allowed to pay someone else to fulfill these religious and civil obligations. Reynaldo told me:

> I am supposed to provide service for my pueblo every three years. They passed me over the first time because at that time I had not yet gone back to my village to get married. However, since so many of us are already living with a woman in the United States they changed the rules. Now if they hear that you have found a woman, you have to accept a *cargo* [literally a load]. So in 1997 it was my turn to be a guardian and helper (*topile*) for the church. Luckily my father, who lives in Mexico, was my replacement; but the second time I had to pay thirty thousand pesos [then about twenty-five hundred dollars] to a cousin in Mexico to act as *comandante* (community policeman).

A man returning for a visit to his hometown, especially if accompanied by his wife, might be asked to take on a more onerous post, such as village mayor (*comisario municipal*) or *fiscal* (treasurer). One cannot pay someone else to take on those duties. Carlos told me what happened a month after his second return visit to Mexico: "I came home with my family to have a rest, to take it easy for a while. But immediately I was told that I had been nominated, and then selected, to be *comisario municipal*." I met Carlos when he was acting in that capacity, which meant presiding over all village council meetings, settling disputes, and representing his community before higher government officials. The position also required him to spend money from his own pocket to entertain visitors. Originally he had planned to stay for only six months, but once he was appointed to this position he remained for a whole year to complete his term of office. Carlos's boss in Los Angeles gave him permission to take more time off work, with the understanding that Carlos's brother would continue to take his place. Migrants cannot afford to cut loose those ties if they want a place to which they can return. Anyone who wants to retain rights to an urban lot in their hometown must provide some form of service or support their home community financially or both. Consequently every undocumented family spends a considerable amount of money to fulfill their duties as citizens of indigenous communities, not to mention the yearly contributions for a big town fiesta. Increasingly stricter border controls, combined with a weaker U.S. economy, are making it ever more difficult for indigenous undocumented workers to fulfill these traditional obligations.

Migrants from indigenous communities in the Alto Balsas have not founded formal organizations in the United States to represent a hometown or region, as have Mixtecos and Zapotecos, two other indigenous groups. However, they do have mutual aid groups, and men from several pueblos have formed bands *(conjuntos)*. Members of these bands perform at private functions and dances that are open to everyone. In the case of migrants from one pueblo (town), now living in several towns near Sacramento, dances are organized to raise money that is sent to Mexico to buy a *castillo* (an elaborate fireworks display). Indeed, there is a dance for each of four barrios (town neighborhoods). In their hometown, barrios have a purely religious function; each barrio has to pay its share of the big annual fiesta in honor of the town's patron saint. Unlike nonindigenous towns in Mexico, the civil authorities are expected to not only attend but participate in such religious events, and all outside visitors are provided with food and alcoholic beverages. The total costs are shared by people living at home as well as migrants, an extra financial burden for indigenous undocumented workers. Consequently any decline in remittances affects not only family members but the entire home community; in 2010, only three *castillos* were lit in the town referred to above.

Family relations, courtship, and marriage are also different for indigenous migrants. In the past, courting couples were strictly chaperoned and had to ask for their parents' permission to marry. Marriage itself was preceded by formal negotiations between representatives of the two families, to make the new union acceptable. That could take several months, even years. If a couple not wanting to wait any longer eloped, they were still required to find an intermediary with the diplomatic skills required to placate the bride's parents. Elopements became more common in Nahua towns during the craft boom and with migration to the United States, but they were still frowned on. However, the last couple of years have seen a change in attitudes. Parents are becoming more accepting of young people living together and now think it is even a good idea for them to get officially married before they leave to go and work in the United States. When living in Mexico in 2001 I witnessed an elopement followed by a set of negotiations. At a meeting set up in the house of the girl's parents it was decided that the couple would live in the apartment of the boy's father who was already in the United States.

It is much easier for young indigenous Mexicans in the United States to date without the scrutiny of parents, especially if one or both parents are living in Mexico. However, once they move in together, they still follow many of the rules that apply in their home village. A good example is Cenobio, the undocumented son of a migrant worker. This young man started to live with the daughter of another migrant who had gone back to Mexico. In the eyes of their parents they had eloped and, according to tradition, one *wewe* or intermediary living in the United States and one in Mexico carried out the necessary negotiations to make sure that both families approved of their union. They received the necessary approval of both sets of parents, but will be expected to have a house built in the village and eventually return to Mexico for a wedding (*boda*).

When the U.S. Census first included the term "Hispanic American Indian," to allow *indígenas* and other Latin American native people to choose this category when filling in the census, some, but certainly not all, people who speak an indigenous language started to choose this ethnic identity. Mexican Americans whose mother tongue is Spanish still look down on *indígenas* or make fun of them, just as they did in Mexico. They might refer to fellow Mexicans from remote rural regions who do not speak Spanish as *indios*, a term with pejorative connotations. At the same time white Americans, who equate race with ethnicity, consider all Mexicans as members of a single group. It is impossible to tell mestizos and *indígenas* apart on the basis of how they look and all Mexicans are equally subject to discrimination in the United States. To muddy the waters even more, indigenous migrants, including most of the undocumented workers from the Alto Balsas, would not consider themselves to be "Indians" the way this group label in used in the United States or Canada. However one has to be careful not to overgeneralize.

Chapter 1 includes a brief overview of the history of Mexico prior to the Spanish conquest when the Nahuatl-speaking Aztecs were the rulers. Today many people in both Mexico and the United States want to revive the customs and religious beliefs associated with the Aztecs and consider themselves to be Meshica. Tourists who visit Mexico City might see Aztec dances performed in the main downtown square, or they might be seen in urban centers in the United States or Europe. Most of these Aztec revivalists are mestizos who have never spoken an indigenous Mexican language. However, based on what I learned during a visit to someone's house in Guerrero, there are at least four people from a town in the Alto Balsas who perform Aztec dances in the United States.

I first met Cirilo in Mexico. He told me he preferred working in Los Angeles (see chapter 7). Cirilo invited me to visit him in his house in Guerrero where we talked at length several days later:

> I first learned about Aztec dances when I saw them performed in the atrium of a church in the Plaza Olvera in Los Angeles. There I spoke to a woman who told me that those dances originated around 1959 in Tlatelolco, Mexico. The dancers included both people from Mexico and Chicanos [Americans of Mexican descent]. Some of the Mexicans even spoke Nahuatl. Later on I joined them in those dances. We danced on the weekend because most of us had to work during the week. They have since come by car to dance in my hometown in Guerrero—but only those who are American citizens or who have work permits.

Albino, whose parents brought him to the United States when he was twelve years old, saw Aztec dancers for the first time in Tijuana, Mexico, and again in 2004 when he attended a big May Day march in Los Angeles. When I visited him at home in Sacramento in 2012, he recalled:

> I told my aunt that I liked those dances and wanted to learn more about them. I now belong to a group of dancers from Sacramento but I am the only one from Guerrero. Most of the dancers are Chicanos born in the U.S. Many do not even speak Spanish, much less Nahuatl, but they have a lot of interest in learning Nahuatl although it is hard to find a good language teacher. Our dance teacher, who does not speak Nahuatl, comes from Mexico City; he trains members of dance groups in Los Angeles, San Francisco, and Chicago. Aztec dances are not folk dances. Every step has a special meaning and participating in those dances is a way of preserving the ideas of our ancestors. The dances are performed in exactly the same way in each city, and some dances require the performers to also sing in Nahuatl.

Albino wanted to create interest in Aztec dances among the people from his home region, but most people are not interested. He told me that the only ones from his hometown who participate are him, his son, and his brother-in-law. But he has not given up creating a greater awareness that all Mexicans share a common indigenous heritage:

> I want my *paisanos* to be proud of their language and their history and not be ashamed of being Meshicas. One day a man who was not aware that I belong to one of the dance groups told me that those who take part in Aztec dances must be crazy and smoke marijuana. When I told him what we do and what we believe in, he realized that what he had told me is not true. He told me, "you are right—those dances are a way of preserving our traditions."

I discovered that some migrants in Texas from another town in the Alto Balsas now see themselves as Aztecs, although they do not perform Aztec dances. They adopted this group identity through contact with the retired American teacher and writer mentioned in the preface. That writer, whose books of fiction deal with the adventures of undocumented children, was surprised that the Nahua migrants she met did not know the history of ancient Mexico. When she learned that they spoke Nahuatl, she told them there were descendants of the Aztecs and showed them books from a museum. This new identity was reinforced when they met a group of Chicanos from a dance group specializing in Aztec dances. Those dancers, affiliated with an American university, discovered there were recent migrants in Houston who spoke Nahuatl when they met the American writer. They subsequently asked a man from the Alto Balsas to give them Nahuatl lessons. This man also now sees himself as an Aztec. Aztec revivalists are the exception rather than the rule in terms of how indigenous migrants from the Alto Balsas identify. However, I anticipate that more of their American-born descendants will also see themselves as Meshicas and carry on the traditions of more ancient ancestors through Aztec dances.

The presence of thousands of *indígenas* from the southern part of Mexico in the United States is a relatively new phenomenon. Yet most native-born Americans not of Mexican descent see them as Mexicans, even if they speak Nahuatl at home. The children of indigenous migrants, on the other hand, see themselves foremost as Americans and their cousins in Mexico call them gringos. Indigenous migrants from Mexico thus face a quandary. How should they fill in the census forms? Who are they?

12

"I Don't Have Much in Common with My Cousin"

Alejandro has two young children who were born in the United States. As American citizens, these children will be able to apply for a passport; they might even end up going to college, as their mother hopes they will. In contrast, the children of Eugenio and Teresa will never have this opportunity. This couple lived together and had two children before emigrating. Those undocumented children, now teenagers, are still not eligible to apply for a driver's license in many of the states where they live, nor will they receive any scholarships. They are likely to do the same kinds of jobs as their parents. In contrast, better educated American-born offspring of undocumented workers who manage to get ahead will not take the kinds of jobs associated with undocumented workers. If enough succeed, the United States will need more workers without work permits— a vicious circle.

The next generation of undocumented workers will not replicate the pattern of circular, intergenerational migration that was prevalent up until the turn of the century. From the 1960s until 1995, the children of most migrant workers were born and raised in Mexico. These children started working in the United States as soon as they were of age. Although these young Mexican-born migrants were undocumented, they were able to go back and forth across a fairly porous U.S. border. They returned to their hometowns to get married, and had their children raised and educated back home, just as their parents had done. This is now rarely the case. Nowadays, young migrants raise their children in the United States. This new trend is creating a social and cultural divide between such children and those born in Mexico. Even if they are related through kinship and common heritage, such children have little in common. Leonardo, the American-born son of one of the documented workers with whom I was staying in California, told me:

> You might have noticed that I do not greet a lot of my neighbors. I do not have much contact with my *paisanos* because I've been living here my whole life. Most of my friends are Americans, including Americans of Mexican descent. I am very different than my cousin Efrain who came here four years ago. We are around the same age but there is little that we can talk about.

Over time, Efrain and Leonardo might get to know each other better if they continue to live in the same place and attend family events. However, they will continue to live in different worlds. Leonardo currently does not have a girlfriend, but I anticipate that he will end up marrying someone with no connections to his hometown. In contrast, Efrain is already married to someone he met in Guerrero. Their taste in music, their aspirations, and the people with whom they associate are different, although they do share the same interest in Latino bands.

I was able to get at least a glimpse into the cross-cultural and intergenerational dynamics of people with roots in the Alto Balsas who now live in the United States, by looking at the messages and pictures they post on Facebook. The writers I recognize are for the most part younger undocumented workers who went to school in Mexico, some of whom are now taking courses in American schools in their spare time. They all use Spanish on the internet, unlike their American-born cousins who write messages in English. You would not know that these Facebook users who write in Spanish are indigenous except when someone occasionally uses a phrase in Nahuatl. Having spent a lot of time in Guerrero I know that the home page on Facebook of one undocumented worker from the Alto Balsas includes a panoramic view of one of the towns in the Alto Balsas. The background of another, more elaborate home page, posted by a young woman educated in Mexico includes a picture of her parents as well as the Mexican Virgen de Guadalupe (the patron saint of Mexico). These young indigenous migrants also share pictures of newborn children or the places they work, share witty comments, and comment on American sport teams. They are gradually becoming Americanized just like their American-born and American-educated cousins.

In chapter 3 we saw how a third of the households in one of the towns where I did my fieldwork do not live in the houses they had built. In doing that exercise I did not try to calculate the number of people now living in the United States who have not yet built, or ever plan to build, a house in Mexico. Second- and third-generation migrants will have little if any contact with a hometown that has little meaning for them. However, people in Mexico will not forget the parents or grandparents of those who will never build houses in towns in the Alto Balsas; this is something I learned while doing my survey. Magdalena and other people who worked on that survey could not tell me much about people they have not seen since they were children, but they certainly know their names and remember their departure.

Migrants from the Alto Balsas who live in places where there are few other migrants have only sporadic contact with people originating in their hometowns. They keep in touch only with very close relatives, usually parents. Once elderly parents, aunts, or uncles die, there is no reason to keep in touch. However, in cities with a concentration of people from the same town in Mexico, especially if they live in the same neighborhood, some level of hometown identity is maintained over several generations. This is the case in California, where a little over a third of the families from the town where I did my survey now live in two large urban centers. Families there regularly rent halls to hold dances and parties, and friends and relatives at home see videos showing such parties. People in Mexico who have never been to the United States thus become acquainted with people they have never met, just by watching those videos. During a phone call with Magdalena in November 2012, I found out that some young couples are now having their weddings in the

United States instead of going back to their hometowns. Her sister-in-law, who had recently seen a video of such a wedding, recognized most of the members of the wedding party and who was dancing with whom. Other people in Mexico viewing the video pointed out which children belonged to which parents, although they wondered whether two couples already had children and who those children might be. Indeed, the purpose of the follow-up work on my survey was to find out whether the children not shown in those videos exist, and whether or not those migrants who have not yet returned married someone originating from their hometown.

In the town where I did my survey, the majority of people left Mexico after 1990, so it was still possible to trace the life histories of all migrants and their descendants. My original list of names included people regardless of where they were born and where they are now living. During subsequent phone calls to Mexico I realized that my original survey could only go so far. My informants could not tell me the number of children of a few couples who have been living in the United States for a long time. In cases where they did know the number of children, they could not come up with their names even when they asked someone else. Nevertheless I managed to come up with a rough estimate of the proportion of descendants of people from this town who are American citizens by virtue of birth. In doing my calculations I took into account the fact that people born in Mexico have much bigger families. It is not unusual for couples in rural Mexico to have as many as ten or twelve children. In contrast, I have yet to encounter a single case of couples in the United States who have more than four children. I thus made the conservative assumption that migrant couples who have been in the United States either since the time they were born, or who themselves grew up in the United States, have an average of three children. I then came up with my figure for the total number of unmarried people, including all those younger than eighteen years old, who were either born in the United States or in Mexico. Forty-four percent of all these children and teenagers are undocumented while the rest (56 percent) were born in the United States. In other words, more than half of the offspring of current undocumented migrants from the town in question are American citizens by virtue of birth. In contrast, prior to 1995 the number of Nahua children born in the United States was miniscule, since their mothers invariably stayed in Mexico. In the case of other towns from the Alto Balsas such as Ameyaltepec, a smaller town where migration is more recent, the proportion of children born in the United States even today would be much lower. For towns like Ahuelican, with a longer history of migration, the proportion of American-born children would be higher, probably well above 60 percent. I suspect that these American descendants of people from the Alto Balsas will be completely erased from the collective memory of those still living in Mexico within a few generations.

Given the complexity of migration patterns of younger couples from the Alto Balsas, some of whom returned home with young children born in the United States, it would be misleading to draw a sharp line between acculturated American-born cousins and their Mexican cousins who do not speak a word of English. In a visit to the town where I did my survey in February 2014, I discovered that twenty-nine children in that town were legally American citizens by virtue of birth. Some of these young Americans, who had come back as babies, and who were just starting grade school, spoke only Nahuatl. In contrast, an older, English-speaking Mexican-born cousin who had attended elementary school in a town in California where no Spanish was spoken either at work or on the street, could barely understand, much less speak, Spanish. He ended up back in Mexico with the whole family after his father was deported. Although this cousin's father had picked up a fair bit of English, both parents had continued to speak to their children in Nahuatl when they were growing up in the United States. This young Mexican citizen was about to start high school in rural Guerrero with very limited Spanish and no knowledge of Mexican history!

The gradual erosion of ties between migrants from the Alto Balsas and most of those they left behind is a more straight-forward process. The small minority of older adults who are "legal" make regular trips back to Mexico, since they have no trouble going back and forth across the border. However, it is not likely that their older children, born and raised in Mexico but now living in the United States, will visit Mexico very often, given the difficulty of reentry with heightened border security. Such undocumented offspring, now established in the United States, will not meet younger brothers or sisters until those siblings in turn arrive in the United States; that is, if they even make it across the border. In contrast, the American-born children of undocumented workers, as U.S. citizens, can easily visit relatives, as long as they or their parents can afford it. The ones whose parents have a more secure income, or those who themselves have jobs, may make one or two tips to Mexico, depending on personal inclination, curiosity, and whether or not their grandparents or other relatives are still alive. However, such visits, usually during their holidays, or to attend the wedding of a close relative, do not constitute durable links with their hometown, and their future children may not even know the name of the place where their grandparents were born.

Almost all the undocumented adult migrants who have not been back to Mexico for many years will have made at least one or two return visits in the past. They would have gone to Mexico for their weddings, or to look at the houses built with the money they sent. A few people have never gone back and may never see Mexico again, including a man who left Mexico as a young man forty years ago. Nevertheless, everyone knows that man and knows that he has a wife and remembers at least some of their children who were born in their hometown. Yet the men and women who rarely or never go back to Mexico generally keep in touch by phone. Those who do not even phone their parents, like the examples mentioned in the introduction, are rare, and can be explained by an earlier breakdown of personal relationships. Undocumented workers cannot afford to completely cut off ties with their hometowns, since they need something on which they can fall back in case anything goes wrong. Their American-born children and grandchildren will still be considered to be members, if not citizens, of their Mexican home communities, but if they stay away too long they will become complete strangers.

The composition of transnational communities is diverse. In chapter 4 we saw how some parents left behind very small children born in Mexico to be cared for by grandparents. Those children will leave their hometowns when they are older, either to the United States or to some other part of Mexico, and some have already done so. Chapter 9 showed how some children whose parents took them across the border when they were very young, as well as those who became Americans by virtue of birth, have gone back for short visits, usually during school holidays. In contrast, undocumented teenagers who are deported rarely end up going back to the United States, and most of them are currently living in the Alto Balsas. These three groups of young people have little in common. Members of the first group are completely bilingual in Spanish and Nahuatl and have spent most of their lives in Mexico. Members of the second group speak Spanish and English, although they would tend to speak mainly English among themselves. For them Mexico is a foreign country where their parents happened to be born, although they can pass as Mexicans. But they are certainly not considered to be *indígenas*. The third Spanish-speaking group, the *cholos*, is more heterogeneous; they have a smattering of English and some can speak Nahuatl, but they are like strangers in their own land where they are neither accepted nor feel at home. I do not know how to categorize another very small group of young people, most of whom are still living in Mexico. They are Americans by virtue of birth, but one or both of their parents took them back to live in the Alto Balsas region when they were still very young, so they received most of their primary education in Mexico. Although they are American citizens, they speak very little or no English. But they will not have any difficulty going back to the United States. However, the majority of younger people who were born and raised in the Alto Balsas will never step foot on Mexican soil because of the militarized border.

"Xkaman Waahloweh" (They Never Come Back)

These words, which I have often heard, are not just part of a saying that belies the fact that quite a few people born in the Alto Balsas actually do end up returning. Deep down in their hearts, people know that migrants do come back, at least sometimes, even though the results are not always happy ones. I chose this expression as the book title because it is consistent with the theme of ambiguity and contradiction inherent in the phenomenon of undocumented workers. The way people in Mexico say "they never come back" is a revelation of the conflicted feelings, sadness, and frustration of those left behind. It also indicates their expectations that people who migrate to earn money by leaving their hometown should come back. It does not matter whether people leave to go off to other parts of Mexico or to the United States. The consensus is that migrants do not come back enough. Those left behind cannot understand why some people rarely or never come home. People who live in Mexico, especially those who have never been in the United States, wish they knew the children and the grandchildren of the people who have emigrated. Magdalena, her sister-in-law, and many other men and women keep hoping that entire migrant families will still come back for visits, the way they often did in the past. When American-born children do come for a visit, they are delighted to find out that some of them can speak Nahuatl. If some of those children do not answer in Nahuatl, they are convinced that they must be able to at least understand their mother tongue, even if that is not the case. They do not realize how little these children have in common with their cousins who were born and raised in Mexico.

The reluctance of the American government to grant work permits, even after NAFTA, combined with a policy of strict border enforcement, while at the same time paying lip service to this policy of border enforcement for more than a decade, has had the unintended consequence that many more children whose parents are Mexican citizens are being born on American soil than would be the case if the United States had not made it more difficult for migrant workers and their family members to cross the border starting around the mid-1990s. If crossing the border had been easier for Mexicans, who would rather go back and forth, there would today be fewer Americans of Mexican descent. Fewer cousins would have ended up becoming almost complete strangers. There would not be as many virtual ghost towns in Mexico today. Ironically, the nativists who harbor anti-immigrant sentiments and who do not want an increase in the number of Spanish-speaking Americans were largely responsible for past failures to reform an immigration policy that has actually been responsible for the huge increase in the Hispanic population in the United States.

13

THE SYSTEM IS BROKEN

The migration of Mexican workers has provided uneven benefits to Mexico. Remittances stimulate house construction and provide additional income for migrant's relatives. On the other hand, regions like the Alto Balsas have experienced decreasing school enrolment and a shortage of people to provide public services. This balance between positive and negative impacts has now started to tilt more to the negative side. During the last downturn of the American economy, undocumented workers sent fewer remittances; the ones I know were barely able to support themselves since they were only able to work for two or three days a week. Yet the pace of migration continued unabated until recently, and those already in the United States are not returning. Increasing continental integration has not resulted in the creation of enough jobs in Mexico to come even close to solving its economic problems. NAFTA was supposed to reduce the differences in wage levels and standards of living between Mexico and the United States, but this is not happening. Different interest groups in the United States want their government to pursue diametrically opposed policies, and the outcome is a system that is not working.

Numerous writers use the word "dysfunctional" to characterize current U.S. immigration policies. Douglas Massey, Jorge Durand, and Nolan Malone have demonstrated that the policy designed between 1986 and 1996 could not have been more dysfunctional. They argue that the system of immigration ran smoothly prior to 1986 and is today hopelessly broken. This dysfunctional system is echoed in the ambiguous situation and conflicted feelings of millions of undocumented migrants, most of whom are from Mexico. Ruth Gomberg-Muñoz writes, "On a broader level, contradictory and confusing U.S. government policy toward unauthorized immigration sends mixed signals to undocumented people." These and other researchers have highlighted the contradictions mentioned in the introduction: that it is inconsistent and unfair to restrict the movement of labor in an increasingly more integrated continental economy. Shannon Gleeson, who has looked at the role of law enforcement agencies, points out another contradiction: the simultaneous efforts of various government agencies to deter and deport undocumented workers, on the one hand, and to protect them from labor abuses such as nonpayment of wages, on the other. The contradictions are even greater today.

Eleven American states, including California, now have laws that allow undocumented workers to apply for a driver's license, although they make it clear that those licenses will not authorize people to work if they do not have a valid work permit. Some Americans do not like those state laws because they are afraid that civil rights advocates will now be able to facilitate the registration of more voters among undocumented workers who use a driver's license as ID. The critics point out a potentially blatant inconsistency that would occur if illegal aliens were allowed to vote in state elections as if they were American citizens. Another example of a contradiction is the outcome of conflicting legal decisions about whether or not undocumented migrants, who were first allowed to study to become lawyers, will be granted licenses, even though they may not be able to make any income by working. One man in Florida, Jose Godinez-Samperio, can, at least for the time being, work legally, but he may not be admitted to the Florida Bar, whereas another man, Sergio C. Garcia of California, can now practice law in that state but cannot earn any income for doing so. Both men were born in Mexico and came to the United States as undocumented immigrants, then attended high school and later graduated from a U.S. law school. Both men are also victims of a combination of discrepancies in the legislation of different states, opposing decisions of state versus federal lawmakers, and the hypocritical and inconsistent nature of U.S. immigration laws.

Garcia is now allowed to practice law in California as a result of the unprecedented ruling by the California Supreme Court on January 2, 2014. However, the U.S. Justice Department opposed Garcia's licensing, while the California Attorney General's Office was in favor of it. The outcome is that Garcia can only provide his legal services for free because he was never granted the green card for which his father had applied nineteen years earlier (in 1995). Sergio Garcia's father, who came to the United States as an undocumented agricultural worker in 1977, had become a legal U.S. resident, and was later granted American citizenship, even though he took his family back to Mexico for eight years. His son, Sergio, crossed the border illegally as a baby and again in 1994 when he was seventeen years old, so he spent most of his childhood in Mexico, where he went to school. In contrast, Jose Godinez-Samperio's parents first brought him across the U.S. border when he was nine years old on a tourist visa that expired. So both Godinez-Samperio and his parents were illegal aliens. However, as of December 2012, Godinez-Samperio has been able to legally work after the Department of Homeland Security authorized the issuance of a Social Security card, a work permit, and continued residency under the Deferred Action for Children Arrivals program resulting from President Obama's decision to halt the deportation process against undocumented immigrants who arrived in the country as children. But Godinez-Samperio cannot practice law in Florida or in any other state (until such time that other states follow the example of California) because the U.S. Department of Justice refused to allow him to be admitted to the Florida Bar because he is not an American citizen. Who knows whether or not anyone from the Alto Balsas who was born in Mexico and later, against all odds, was admitted to an American law school, even though he or she is undocumented, will ever be allowed to practice as a U.S. attorney. That is not likely to happen without comprehensive immigration reform at the federal level.

Why the Broken System Needs to Be Fixed

The current situation does not make sense. Even Republican members of a group of eight senators who proposed a bipartisan bill to reform the U.S.

immigration system in the summer of 2013 used the label "broken" to describe the old system. Regardless of how one feels about the neoliberal philosophy advocated by conservative politicians, this economic theory has not been consistently applied. It is not consistent to advocate free markets and open competition but not the free movement of workers across borders. The labor market should also be free; instead, a neoliberal free trade agreement was followed by an increasingly militarized border to deter migrant workers. One proposed way to make current policies consistent would be to change U.S. federal law based on the Fourteenth Amendment to the U.S. Constitution, which mandates that all those born in the United States are citizens, so that children of migrant workers born in the United States would not automatically become U.S. citizens. In the short run such a draconian measure would increase the number of undocumented people but it would also remove an incentive for future migrant workers to have children in the United States. But that kind of legislation goes completely against the notion of America as a land of immigrants working hard to create a better future for their children and a place of opportunity for all those born on its soil. It is a paradox that the U.S. government would have to go against its own principles to fix a broken system of immigration. The presence of so many undocumented migrants, including their Mexican-born children, and the rapidly growing number of American-born children of such migrants, is a quandary for American society.

One could use a moral argument that gives priority to the principle of fairness, rather than one based strictly on the grounds of logical consistency. It is unfair that the U.S. government has set aside a miniscule number of work visas for Mexico, considering Mexico's large population. Furthermore, no one likes the hypocrisy of a policy that results in a huge gap between labor standards and how those standards are enforced, particularly in the case of the more vulnerable workforce of undocumented workers. Gleeson points out that the presence of migrants deemed to be illegal is paradoxical because under American law their rights as workers need to be protected, even though in theory they are here illegally. She points out that the majority of undocumented workers are never detained or deported, yet occasional raids and deportations "send a chilling reminder to all workers who labor in the shadows that their place in U.S. society is precarious." The current situation of restricting the entry of migrant workers goes against the image of the United

States as a country that once opened its arms to those who want to fulfill their dreams.

From the perspective of those interested in social justice, we need to take into consideration the rights of people to make a decent living. The insecurity of not having legal status and the fact that their labor rights are unprotected makes undocumented workers vulnerable to exploitation, as demonstrated by Judith Hellman. Up until about ten years ago the large industrial labor unions were opposed to legalizing undocumented workers. They thought migrant workers took away jobs from American workers and were the main cause of lower wages. Even the United Farm Workers (UFW), cofounded by the Mexican American Cesar Chavez, was originally hostile to undocumented farmworkers. It even supported the cancellation of the bracero program in 1964. But labor advocates have since adopted a very different position; today they support immigration reform and would like to do more to support undocumented workers. The AFL-CIO, the largest union federation in the United States, opposed NAFTA precisely because the agreement did not go far enough to incorporate basic labor standards that would be applied to both Mexico and the United States.

Setting aside the concerns of those who want to see social justice, as well as issues of morality and national image, there are lots of practical economic reasons why the system needs to be fixed. Massey, Durand, and Malone's book provides evidence that the free movement of people between countries with different standards of living and wages will in the long run result in a closing of the gap. The book uses the successful integration of Portugal and Spain into the European Union as a model, showing that at the end of economic unification both countries experienced a net return of migration from northern Europe. Little further migration from those southern European countries occurred and the number of migrants who had gone to work in places such as Germany, the Netherlands, and France and who then returned was greater than the number of people who continued to migrate to northern Europe. Massey and his coauthors use this example to argue that a new immigration policy based on sound economic principles would lead to long-term reductions in the influx of workers from Mexico. They include figures that show that it takes about ninety years to reduce the gap in living standards and wages between neighboring countries to any significant extent. Other researchers calculate that one-way migration slows down only when differences in wages reach about five to one, instead of ten to one, which is currently the case of the United States compared to Mexico.

Massey and his coauthors argue that up to now the immigration policies of the United States have been counterproductive. The facts and figures in their 2002 study show that a restrictive border policy has only discouraged migrants from returning home, thus transforming a system of seasonal migration into one of permanent settlement. A study by Florian Kaufmann, published in 2011, has confirmed these findings. There are other reasons for fixing the system. A policy that makes it easier for Mexican workers to enter the United States would mean that the drug cartels currently involved in smuggling people across the border, as a side business to smuggling drugs, would lose much of their income. A more open border will also result in a higher rate of involvement of migrants in organizations dedicated to improving the infrastructure of their hometowns in Mexico. Robert C. Smith's book on Mexican migrants of Mixteca descent from the state of Puebla demonstrates how an international committee whose members raised funds in New York made substantial contributions to such public projects in Mexico as piped drinking water and high schools. The committee even influenced the outcome of local Mexican elections in a positive way. However, this committee was run by men who had work permits, residency, and in some cases even U.S. citizenship; those men started migrating much earlier, well before the 1986 amnesty. In contrast, the emigration of indigenous people from the Alto Balsas started much later. For them, stricter border controls hinder or reduce, rather than foster, transnational life.

Transnationalism and Assimilation

Transnational is a word used by today's scholars of migration; they use such terms as transnational citizenship, transnational community, and transborder lives to refer to the involvement of migrants in the politics and social life of both their country of origin and their country of destination. Writers using such terms also point out that it is possible, and even desirable, to be *indígena*, Mexican, and American at the same time. They do not think that international migration inevitably leads to a loss of cultural practices and past loyalties. Robert Smith, who uses the term "transnational life," sees transnationalism as an ongoing process. In his study of Mexican migrants in New York, he explores different aspects of transnational life at the local level, looking at how people of different ages experience transnational life. Smith includes examples of young people, including second-generation, American-born migrants who went back to their parents' hometown to attend religious festivals, which in turn changed how they saw themselves. I found similar cases in my case study. As in the case of Puebla, gang members whose parents came from the Alto Balsas also ended up returning to Mexico, which then changed patterns of violence in their hometowns, as we saw in chapter 10.

One manifestation of transnational life is small businesses specializing in money transfers or transporting Mexican goods desired by Mexicans working in the United States. Such enterprises allow people who would rather live in Mexico to combine the better of two worlds. Judith Hellman uses the example of return migrants in Zacatecas who are now growing prickly pears and other fruits in Zacatecas to be exported to the United States where there is a huge demand for such nostalgic Mexican food. Such migrants first have to work in the United States long enough to accumulate the capital needed to set up a business that then allows them to spend a good part of the year in Mexico. But the only way to carry out their plans is to have the residency status needed to go back and forth freely. An example from the Alto Balsas is Pancho, one of the few documented migrants mentioned in chapter 5. He invested in a truck used to transport Mexican cheese and dried meat to several cities in California, as well as delivering packages. He also spent the money he earned in the United States to make improvements to his ranch in Mexico, which produces the milk used to make cheese, and to buy traditional clothing that is made only in Mexico. Any future growth in the economy is bound to open up more opportunities for such small transborder enterprises. Issuing more permits that allow migrants to make multiple border crossings, and, even better, providing opportunities for undocumented workers who wish to do so to become American citizens, would enhance this facet of transnational life. All these cases illustrate that assimilation and transnationalism are not mutually exclusive.

Assimilation is not an inevitable process of Mexican immigrants becoming just like other Americans in the United States, or *indígenas* in Mexico becoming mestizos. We have seen how indigenous migrants from Mexico may become more like other Mexicans in the United States, as well as becoming more like Americans in some regards. At the same time, migrants from the Alto Balsas and other indigenous regions in Mexico are also playing a role in the reshaping of American culture, as shown by the emergence of a new definition of what it means to be a Native American or "Indian." Smith draws a further distinction between two kinds of assimilation: negative assimilation associated with quitting school and entering dead-end jobs versus positive assimilation involving more schooling and better jobs. He argues that return visits by young people to their hometowns, and their involvement in Mexican hometown associations founded by their parents, has the potential of enhancing positive assimilation, although some forms of transnationalism such as transborder gangs could contribute to greater negative assimilation in both the United States and Mexico. I would go further to argue that the type of transnational life associated with being documented is more likely to lead to positive assimilation, whereas both undocumented youth and the offspring of undocumented migrants are more likely to experience negative assimilation. This is one more reason for immigration reform resulting in fewer undocumented people living and working in the United States.

The ongoing debates about immigration reform indicate a lack of awareness of the process of transnationalism, and of the reality of the transborder lives of people with strong links to both Mexico and the United States. This lack of sensitivity is reflected in the word "alien," a legal term with negative connotations used to refer to anyone who is not an American citizen, including the Canadians and Mexicans who are supposed to be friends and equal partners in a single integrated continental economy. Even advocates for immigration reform assume that all immigrants, including nonimmigrant workers who are lawfully admitted to the United States, want to become American citizens and then live the rest of their lives there. They assume that they will end up thinking and acting just like other English-speaking Americans. This assumption is evident in the use of the term "registered provisional immigrants" included in current proposals for immigration reform. A poll conducted in April 2013 by Latino Decisions shows that a high percentage of the undocumented people (87 percent) said they wanted to become citizens if allowed to do so under an immigration reform. However, one should not overlook that a large number of undocumented migrants, particularly if they are over the age of thirty and were raised in Mexico, would prefer the option of maintaining their Mexican citizenship if given the choice. In her book on Mexican migrants Judith Hellman debunks the notion that all immigrants want to become full-fledged Americans. Migrants born and raised in Mexico have strong attachments to their communities of origin, and many of them are more interested in maintaining contact with those communities while earning money in the United States. Many Mexican migrants who cross the border would eventually like to go back to retire, or would prefer a good job in Mexico. In contrast, the children of migrant families who were raised and educated in the United States, regardless of whether or not they are American citizens by birth, are not so keen to spend a lot of time in Mexico, much less become Mexican citizens. However, in the United States they are still subject to racial stereotyping. To ensure their successful integration into American life, and economic success, will require reforms to an educational system that currently does not meet the needs of Latinos and other disadvantaged groups. As pointed out by Robert Smith, too few Americans of Latino descent have the college education required in a modern, technologically more advanced society.

Why Has the System Not Been Fixed Yet?

Given the dire need for immigration reform, one wonders why the system has not yet been fixed, and why current attempts to change the law face an uphill battle. The main obstacle to the implementation of a viable solution is not a dearth of information and ideas, but the absence of anything even close to a consensus among groups with competing interests and values. So far, every attempt to deal with problems associated with the current lack of labor market mobility has failed. The obsession with national security after the events of 9/11, resulting in the formation of the Department of Homeland Security, as well as the current worldwide recession, did not help matters. Several earlier proposals for immigration reform presented in Congress were rejected by both immigration advocates and anti-immigrant groups. It looks as if the current initiatives for immigration reform, spearheaded and even approved in the U.S. Senate, will not be passed by Congress. If only bits and pieces of the proposals that originated in the Senate, probably with an emphasis on a more militarized border, become law, the system will become even more dysfunctional.

It is extremely ironic that, between the 1930s and the ratification of the NAFTA agreement in 1993, there was no free trade, with hefty tariff protections for industry on the Mexican side, yet the border was practically open in terms of the movement of labor. Today, with free trade and an almost completely integrated continental economy, there is very little freedom for Mexican workers to go back and forth between Mexico and the United States. The broken system cannot be fixed unless the basic contradictions of free trade, combined with the lack of a free market for international labor, are resolved. I agree with the argument of Massey and his collaborators on the need for a new philosophy. Much has changed since 2002 when they came up with a set of policy solutions, but their assumption is still valid; namely, that international migration is not a pathological condition to be stamped out, but rather a natural outcome of the entry of less developed countries into a new global economy.

The latest plans to continue building more fences and holding facilities for detainees, as well as better electronic sensors, are a clear indication that American immigration policy is still based on false assumptions. Even more stringent border controls and an increasingly militarized border might very well close legal immigration to all but a small number of Mexican workers. That is already happening. Who knows what might be the outcome of this bad policy? Unfortunately, the situation is at an impasse. Ironically, American citizens who put greater emphasis on free enterprise and fewer regulations, and who are therefore more inclined to vote for the Republican Party, may be inclined to vote for the Democrats, even if they do not like that party's political philosophy, once they realize that is the only way to ensure the immigration reforms needed to guarantee America's prosperity. This is unlikely to happen, given the partisan nature of American politics. For the same reasons many Democrats might block any attempt at immigration reform if a Republican president again wanted to implement immigration reform along the lines originally proposed by George W. Bush. That proposal, which was opposed by the majority of Republicans, was not ideal, because it put an emphasis on stricter border controls. However, that proposal did include the possibility of a blanket amnesty for the majority of undocumented immigrants already in the United States and more work permits for Mexicans who want to work in the United States. In his January 28, 2008, State of the Union address to Congress, President Bush said, "We will never fully secure our border until we create a lawful way for foreign workers to come here and support our economy." Unfortunately, he was not successful in getting his proposal through Congress.

The ongoing competing interests of American business and American politicians, most of whom are more interested in staying in power than in finding a practical solution, might yet end up resulting in the continual decline, and eventually the collapse, of the U.S. economy—in large part because it will no longer be easy to have access to the Mexican migrant workers needed to keep the U.S. economy competitive. Once the international economy rebounds, as it has done in the past, there will be an even greater need for Mexican labor in the United States. American businesses will demand access to more migrant labor. If not enough American citizens are available, especially for unskilled jobs, they will have no other choice but to continue recruiting undocumented workers, no matter how many fines are imposed. Nor will Mexicans stop looking for ways to work in the United States, at least for another decade, even if the restructured Mexican economy experiences further economic growth. Without a real change in immigration policy, both the economic and the political situation will get worse rather than better.

What Can Be Done to Fix the System?

A new immigration policy will not work in the long run unless it can help both the United States and Mexico, as well as Canada, to develop stronger economies. The purpose of continental integration is to allow North America to become more competitive with other parts of the world. The United States will never become more competitive on its own, especially if it restricts the free flow of labor within that continent. In order to nurture a strong and competitive continental economy, the United States will need Mexico's labor as much as Mexico needs further investment from both the United States and Canada. To be truly successful, continental economic integration needs to go hand in hand with the right kind of immigration policies, whose implementation will in the long term result in a state of affairs where Mexico no longer loses a large proportion of its working population to out-migration, and where people of Mexican descent living in the United States will no longer feel that they do not belong to American society. Such an outcome will require both short-term and long-term solutions.

A doable short-term solution to the problem of the existence of undocumented Mexican workers in the United States would be something resembling the amnesty program approved by Congress and signed by President Ronald Reagan in 1986. Such a program should make it possible for undocumented workers without a criminal record, and who have been in the United States for at least three years, to apply for residency status. Those with residency status would not only be able to legally work in the United States but could also go back and forth to Mexico. Such a proposal, which would also allow migrant workers to apply for full citizenship status, is again being considered today. The advantage of U.S. citizenship for undocumented Mexican adults who have a strong attachment to Mexico is that it would enable them to be more connected to their homeland, including the freedom to travel and stay there more often. Ideally such people should be able to opt for dual citizenship. However, to only allow undocumented workers to apply for legal status from within the United States, as was done with the 1986 immigration reform law, will not work unless a reasonable number of permits can be simultaneously issued to citizens from both Mexico and the Central American countries who will still want to enter the American labor market. Any quotas for visas and work permits should be sufficient to meet the future demands of the U.S. labor market. The failure to issue sufficient work permits to meet the labor needs of the American economy will inevitably lead to an influx of an even larger number of new undocumented workers, just like what happened after the last amnesty. If a very expensive and highly militarized U.S. border were to succeed in curtailing such an influx, the North American economy will not have the competitive edge it needs to survive in the broader global system.

A dual proposal that involvers the legalization of current undocumented workers and the issuing of more work permits to new migrants would be the first step in much longer process culminating in the true integration of the economies of equal partners. In the short term the U.S. economy will still need additional migrant labor. Mexico, our current NAFTA partner with its already well-developed networks of migrants, is the logical source of such labor. Given the discrepancies in current wages and living standards between these two countries, the best way of regulating the natural flow of migrants is some form of circular migration program as recommended by experts such as Massey, Wayne Cornelius, Jessa Lewis, and Kaufmann. They have already demonstrated that such a program, which could take the form of a guest worker program, is in the best interests of both Mexico and the United States. If entire families of Mexican migrants were to come and stay in the United States, as they are currently forced to do, Mexico will not have a sufficient number of young people whose skills and energy are needed for its future economic development. The departure of whole families, instead of just individual family members who come and go, puts a greater burden on Mexico because of the resulting loss of remittances, which are still crucial to the Mexican economy. Migrant workers who need to support their families in the United States, which is much more expensive than if their younger children were in Mexico, have less money to send to Mexico. Even the old U.S. system of halfhearted border enforcement, which facilitated a form of circular migration, would be better than the current proposal to make it ever more difficult and riskier for the Mexican workers needed to assure a strong North American economy to cross the border.

Whatever form it takes, some form of circular migration system along the lines of a guest worker program should be an interim, temporary measure on the way to the final goal of creating a North American market that includes the free flow of labor, which should go both ways and not just northward. Kaufmann's position is that both governments need to agree that a guest worker program will have to be phased out in the long run, concomitant with the creation of more and better jobs in Mexico. In the meantime complementary policies that are internally consistent and will not lead to new contradictions are required. A new guest worker program will need to be carefully designed and implemented in such a manner that the rights of workers are as important as the needs of employers. Shannon Gleeson advocates the proper enforcement of laws related to immigrant workers, including the enforcement of wage and hours laws. Massey puts more emphasis on the need for more inspections to enforce existing labor, health, and safety laws, pointing out that effective enforcement would remove the incentive to hire undocumented workers as a way for employers to get around those laws, as they do under the current situation where enforcement is almost nonexistent. But to ensure that employers of documented workers follow the rules will require the diversion of resources now used for border enforcement.

The involvement of labor unions is another component of the solution. The U.S. government, as well as large employers, have so far put too many roadblocks in the way of labor unions whose influence and power is probably the lowest of any Western industrialized nation. The fact that unions are now on board in terms of their willingness to organize and help undocumented workers is a good sign, but they need to muster more grassroots support from Americans before they can effectively influence public policy. Historically labor unions have been largely responsible for achieving better incomes and benefits. However, the fact that they currently represent less than 15 percent of workers, who on average earn 10 to 30 percent more than nonunionized workers, will make it harder to convince the majority of Americans that they are effective advocates for the working poor. If labor activists succeed in mobilizing both documented and undocumented workers in a wide range of industries, the same way that Cesar Chavez organized Mexican and Filipino farmworkers in the 1960s, they might yet be able to play an effective role in ensuring the enforcement of safety standards and in making that the wages of the bottom half of the population, including immigrant workers, are not eroded even further.

Additional proposals for immigration reform presented in Douglas Massey's 2012 book, as well as other ideas put forward by more recent critics of U.S. immigration policy, are still valid. For example, it would be a good idea to charge migrants applying for work visas five hundred dollars to cover administrative costs. Mexican migrants would be happy to pay a price to enter the American workforce that is much lower than what they now have to pay to coyotes, as noted by Hellman. Kaufmann has commented on the continued importance of the Mexican government's outreach programs to ease the return and reintegration of migrants, as well as programs to stimulate migrant investment in Mexico by matching any funds raised by migrant organizations in the United States for community projects in migrants' hometowns.

Mexico will still be dependent on the remittances of migrant workers for at least a few more decades. The process of legalization, combined with a new guest worker program, will result in an increase of such remittances. In contrast, the current policies, which have led to entire families of undocumented workers staying permanently in the United States, actually mean a decrease in remittances. A guest worker program that allows legal migrant workers to move back and forth across the border will avoid this from happening again. When migrant workers reorient themselves to the United States, as they are forced to do today, their economic and social ties to Mexico are weakened. They will end up sending less money to their home communities. We have seen how the American-born children of undocumented workers no longer help to stimulate the local economy by having houses built. It is no wonder the Mexican government is making efforts to strengthen migrants' identification with Mexico and to foster their attachment to home communities. However, to accelerate the process leading to a narrower gap between the economies of the United States and Mexico, the American government will also have to allocate part of its foreign aid budget for improvements in Mexico's infrastructure and its social programs. Kaufmann, Raul Delgado, and Luis Eduardo Guarnizo all believe that it is in the best interest of the United States to partner with the Mexican government as well as the private sector to ensure the further development of the Mexican economy. To reach the goal of a comprehensive immigration reform requires a long-term perspective including a multilateral partnership for Mexican development. Reducing the flow of migrant workers without closing the gap in income between neighboring countries will be counterproductive, as aptly summarized by Kaufmann: "As permanent depression of the U.S. economy seems hardly the preferred way to cut Mexican migration inflows, it is in the interest of the U.S. government to partner with the Mexican government, private sector, and migrants to support economic development in Mexico."

It will not be easy to bring about meaningful changes in the U.S. system of immigration, but it is never too late to act. Compromises will have to be made in order to get the necessary legislation passed, given the polarization of political opinion in the United States. The biggest challenge for overcoming the current impasse is to convince the majority of American citizens of the need for a radical overhaul of the old, now dysfunctional system. Recent polls indicate that two-thirds of Americans, including a majority of Republicans, already support a path to citizenship for undocumented workers, whereas only 20 percent support deportation alone (which is the policy today). Many states are already passing their own legislation to protect the rights of immigrants now living in the United States, as we have seen.

American citizens will have to do more lobbying plus use their votes to put pressure on legislators to do the right thing. Much of the legislation is already there, ready to be approved. Once passed, it will not be easy to implement a new set of coherent policies; to fix the broken system will require more than the right kind of legislation by the federal government. New laws and regulations only provide an overall framework. As pointed out by Gleeson, their successful implementation will depend on the cooperation of both national governments as well as the coordination of local governments, various state agencies, humanitarian organizations, political advocacy groups, and foreign consulates.

Final Remarks

What struck me most in doing the research for this book is the sense of loss, futility, and ambivalence that came up time and time again in my interviews. When I first met Delfino in Mexico in 2006 I asked him about what he wanted in life:

> I know what I want. I want to go back to the U.S. where I plan to finish my schooling and then find a job. My goal is to build a big house here in Mexico; I want a driveway and two cars [he joked that one would be for him and one for his future wife]. I want ceramic tiles in all of the rooms. When I am older, I want to live here in that house with my wife and children. I would like them to learn Nahuatl.

When I later asked him whether his children would be likely to ever live in Mexico, he realized that his wishes were unrealistic, that they were only dreams:

> When I have children I know they will only be able to make a good living in the States. I want them to do well and be happy, and maybe they will help me when I am old. But I also want them to come and visit my village. I do not really know what will happen to us in the future.

Delfino's future children will probably end up among those who "never come back." His conflicting goals, to earn more money, to have children, and for those children to get to know the town he loves so much, echo a huge contradiction: an integrated, economic system in North America has generated a greater demand for Mexican workers yet the U.S. government will not allow more workers across the border. The migrant workers already in the United States who need or want to go back for visits to their homes in Mexico are finding it increasingly difficult to reenter. At the same time there are not enough jobs in Mexico so Mexicans will keep trying to enter the United States. Yet the few undocumented who succeed in crossing the border will not be able fulfill their dreams. As the inhabitants of a continent that stretches from the Arctic to the Panama Canal, we who live north of the Rio Grande need to listen to the stories of our southern neighbors. Together the three governments who signed the NAFTA agreement need to address the contradictions inherent in the system and thus make it possible for everyone to have a better life.

Suggested Readings and References

For anyone interested in reading books similar to *They Never Come Back* I recommend Judith Adler Hellman's *The World of Mexican Migrants: The Rock and the Hard Place* (2008). It is about Mexican migrants, including undocumented workers, using lots of examples based on interviews she conducted in five locations in the United States and another five in Mexico. I refer to her study, as well as to the work of several other authors, in my book on undocumented workers. Hellman has also written several books on Mexico, including *Mexican Lives* (1994) and *Mexico in Crisis* (1983). For a book that looks specifically at indigenous migrants in the United States one can refer to the volume edited by Jonathan Fox and Gaspar Rivera-Salgado, *Indigenous Mexican Migrants in the United States* (2004). That collection of readings deals with hometown associations and the political mobilization of Mixtec and Zapotec people from Oaxaca, Mexico. Another book that deals with indigenous migrants is Lynn Stephen's *Transborder Lives* (2007). Her study mainly deals mainly with agricultural workers, as does the Fox volume. A study that focuses exclusively on indigenous migrants in a large urban setting is that of Jacqueline Maria Hagan, *Deciding to Be Legal* (1994). Her book includes many observations about the workplace experience and housing of a group of people from Guatemala. The focus of her book is the process of legalization of earlier migrants. For those interested in the experiences of Mexican migrants in New York, I recommend Robert Smith's *Mexican New York* (2006), a study focusing on the transnational lives of three generations of Mexicans in New York. His book explores many aspects of a more established community of people who came from a Spanish-speaking town in the state of Puebla that has indigenous (Mixteca) features. For an up-to-date ethnography of undocumented workers in Chicago I recommend Ruth Gomberg-Muñoz's *Labor and Legality* (2011).

Books about migration from Mexico in general and case studies looking at the links between Mexico and the United States, including studies of border enforcement, are too numerous to mention all of them. A good place to start are the publications distributed by, or on behalf of, the Center for Comparative Immigration Studies (CCIS), such as *Impacts of Border Enforcement on Mexican Migration: the View from Sending Communities*, a book coedited by Wayne A. Cornelius and Jessa M. Lewis (2007). This center has also put out numerous ethnographic surveys of sending communities that have satellite communities in the United States, including communities from the predominantly indigenous Mexican Mixteca region (see also Cornelius et al. 2009). A book that deals specifically with the topic of policing the border is Peter Andreas's *Border Games* (2009). It includes a comparison between the United States and eastern Europe, while David Spencer's *Clandestine Crossings* (2009) focuses on migrants and coyotes. Joanna Derby's *Divided by Borders: Mexican Migrants and Their Children* (2010) covers the family dynamics of Mexican migrants. For an analysis of hometown associations I recommend an article by Luin Goldring, "The Mexican State and Transmigrant Organizations" (2002). Smith and Bakker's *Citizenship across Borders* (2008) includes a discussion of transnational research, as does Stephen's study of indigenous Oaxacans in Mexico, California, and Oregon (2007) whose central themes are the politics of translocality, transnational politics, and transnational citizenship. These last two books, as well as Smith's study of migrants in New York, include bibliographical references for those interested in tracing back the use of the term "transnational." In one of my earlier publications,

"The Alto Balsas Nahuas," I use of the term "transnational indigeneity" (see Schryer 2010a).

There are thousands of books about the history of Mexico, including the history of ethnic relations between mestizos and *indígenas*. My treatment of the history of Mexico in this book follows a fairly standard interpretation, but elsewhere I put more emphasis on the crucial roles played by a class of farmers called rancheros at the time of the Mexican Revolution (see Schryer 1980). In two other publications I point out that that rancheros (generally thought to be mestizos) can also be *indígenas* (see Schryer 1990, 1997). For a now classic anthropological treatment I recommend Eric Wolf's *Sons of the Shaking Earth* (1959).

Readers who want to learn more about the Alto Balsas region of Guerrero, Mexico, will not encounter many books or articles available in English. Jonathan Amith (1995) put together a collection of articles with lots of illustrations. Most of the chapters in that volume deal with the tradition of *amate* painting, while the first chapter provides information on the archeology of the region. There are references to some towns in the Alto Balsas in his *The Möbius Strip*, a book that deals mainly with the colonial history of the valley of Iguala (see Amith 2005). Tyler Cowen's *Markets and Cultural Voices* (2005) looks at the craft industry from the perspective of an economist who did extensive interviews with several of the best known *amate* painters. For those who can read Spanish or French, most of the foreign language material on the region is included in the bibliographies of several chapters I have written for edited volumes (see Schryer 2010a, 2010b). A book written in Spanish that provides a comprehensive coverage of the craft industry was written by the anthropologist Catherine Good Eshelman (1988) who did most of her fieldwork in Ameyaltepec, Guerrero. For those who read German, I recommend a book by Henry Kammler (2010), which includes references to migratory workers in Houston.

For an overview of the history of Mexican immigrant and Mexican Americans, with an emphasis on the politics of ethnicity, one can read David Gutierrez's *Wall and Mirrors* (1995). Douglas S. Massey, Jorge Durand, and Nolan J. Malone's *Beyond Smoke and Mirrors* (2002) deals more specifically with what is wrong with the American system of immigration, including a set of policy recommendations. They compare the system of migration to an intricate machine with moving parts that need to fit well together, explaining how this machine worked well in the past. Their central argument is that the system got clogged up and stopped running smoothly as a result of a series of bad decisions by policymakers. The economist Florian K. Kaufman (2011) comes to a similar conclusion in a more technical book that came out of a PhD dissertation. Shannon Gleeson's *Conflicting Commitments* (2012) applies the concept of "social field," developed by the French sociologist Pierre Bourdieu, to examine the politics of enforcing immigrant worker rights. For those readers interested in a book written by a well-known journalist, I recommend David Bacon's *Illegal People* (2008).

References

Amith, Jonathan D. 1995. *The Amate Tradition: Innovation and Dissent in Mexican Art.* Chicago: Mexican Fine Arts Center Museum.

——. 2005. *The Möbius Strip: A Spatial History of Colonial Society in Guerrero, Mexico.* Stanford: Stanford University Press.

Andreas, Peter. 2009. *Border Games: Policing the U.S.-Mexico Divide.* 2nd ed. Ithaca: Cornell University Press.

Bacon, David. 2008. *Illegal People: How Globalization Created Migration and Criminalized Immigrants.* Boston: Beacon Press.

Cornelius, Wayne A., David Scott Fitzgerald, Jose Hernández-Díaz, and Scott Berger, eds. 2009. *Migration from the Mexican Mixteca: A Transnational Community in Oaxaca and California.* CCIS Anthologies. La Jolla: University of California, San Diego, Center for Comparative Immigration Studies.

Cornelius, Wayne A., and Jessa M. Lewis, eds. 2007. *Impacts of Border Enforcement on Mexican Migration: The View from Sending Communities.* La Jolla: CCIS Anthologies, vol. 6. La Jolla: University of California, San Diego, Center for Comparative Immigration Studies.

Cowen, Tyler. 2005. *Markets and Cultural Voices: Liberty vs. Power in the Lives of Mexican Amate Painters.* Ann Arbor: University of Michigan Press.

Delgado, Raul, and Luis Eduardo Guarnizo. 2007. "Migration and Development: Lessons from the Mexican Experience." Washington, DC: Migration Policy Institute.

Derby, Joanna. 2010. *Divided by Borders: Mexican Migrants and Their Children.* Berkeley: University of California Press.

Fox, Jonathan, and Gaspar Rivera-Salgado, eds. 2004. *Indigenous Mexican Migrants in the United States.* San Diego: University of California, San Diego, Center for U.S.-Mexican Studies/Center for Comparative Immigration Studies.

Gleeson, Shannon. 2012. *Conflicting Commitments: The Politics of Enforcing Immigrant Worker Rights in San Jose and Houston.* Ithaca: Cornell University Press.

Goldring, Luin. 2002. "The Mexican State and Transmigrant Organizations: Negotiating the Boundaries of Membership and Participation in the Mexican Nation." *Latin American Research Review* 37, no. 3: 55–99.

Gomberg-Muñoz, Ruth. 2011. *Labor and Legality: An Ethnography of a Mexican Immigration Network*. New York: Oxford University Press.

Good Eshelman, Catherine 1988. *Haciendo la lucha (arte y comercio nahuas de Guerrero)*. México: Fondo de Cultural Económica.

Gutierrez, David G. 1995. *Walls and Mirrors: Mexican Americans, Mexican Immigrants and the Politics of Ethnicity*. Berkeley: University of California Press.

Hagan, Jacqueline María. 1994. *Deciding to Be Legal: A Mayan Community in Houston*. Philadelphia: Temple University Press.

Hellman, Judith Adler. 1983. *Mexico in Crisis*. 2nd rev. ed. New York: Holmes & Meier.

———. 1994. *Mexican Lives*. New York: New Press.

———. 2008. *The World of Mexican Migrants: The Rock and the Hard Place*. New York: New Press.

Kammler, Henry. 2010. *Kulturwandel und die Konkurrez der Religionen in Mexico: Nahuas in Guerrero zwischen der Herrschaft der Winde und der Macht des Wortes*. Stuttgart: Kohlhammer Druckerei.

Kaufmann, Florian K. 2011. *Mexican Labor Migration and U.S. Immigration Policies: From Sojourners to Emigrants?* El Paso: LFB Scholarly Publishing.

Massey, Douglas S., Jorge Durand, and Nolan J. Malone. 2002. *Beyond Smoke and Mirrors: Mexican Immigration in an Era of Economic Integration*. New York: Russell Sage Foundation.

Schryer, Frans J. 1980. *The Rancheros of Pisaflores: The Case History of a Peasant Bourgeoisie in Twentieth Century Mexico*. Toronto: University of Toronto Press.

———. 1990. *Ethnicity and Class Conflict in Rural Mexico*. Princeton: Princeton University Press.

———. 1997. "Rancheros." In *The Encyclopaedia of Mexico*, vol. 2, edited by Michael Werner, 1235–37. Chicago: Fitzroy Dearborn Publishers.

———. 2010a. "The Alto Balsas Nahuas: Transnational Indigeneity and Interactions in the World of Art and Crafts, the Politics of Resistance, and the Global Labor Market." In *Indigenous Cosmopolitans: Transnational and Transcultural Indigeneity in the Twenty-First Century*, edited by Maximilian C. Forte, 97–125. New York: Peter Lang.

———. 2010b. "Globalization and *Indígenas*: The Alto Balsas Nahuas." In *Latin American Identities after 1980*, edited by Gordana Yovanovich and Amy Huras, 51–78. Waterloo, Ontario: Wilfrid Laurier Press.

Smith, Michael Peter, and Matt Bakker. 2008. *Citizenship across Borders: The Political Transnationalism of El Migrante*. Ithaca: Cornell University Press.

Smith, Robert Courtney. 2006. *Mexican New York: Transnational Lives of New Immigrants*. Berkeley: University of California Press.

Spencer, David. 2009. *Clandestine Crossings: Migrants and Coyotes on the Texas-Mexico Border*. Ithaca: Cornell University Press.

Stephen, Lynn. 2007. *Transborder Lives: Indigenous Oaxacans in Mexico, California, and Oregon*. Durham, NC: Duke University Press.

Telles, Edward E., and Vilma Ortiz. 2008. *Generations of Exclusion: Mexican Americans, Assimilation, and Race*. New York: Russell Sage Foundation.

Wolf, Eric. 1959. *Sons of the Shaking Earth*. Chicago: University of Chicago Press.

Acknowledgments

I am grateful for the help I have received from all the people I got to know in Guerrero as well as in the United States, including the retired teacher and writer already mentioned in this book. I cannot use your real names in order to protect those who are undocumented. I would not have been able to do the research to write this book without your cooperation, including driving me around, taking me with you on numerous visits, letting me stay in your homes, and giving me recommendations to talk to people I did not know. You have all been generous with your time. My many friends in Mexico opened their doors when I showed up unexpectedly, sometimes early in the morning or very late at night. Thank you. Muchas gracias. Tlaxtlawe!

I want to acknowledge the contribution of my brother Herman Schryer, who meticulously copyedited the first two drafts of the manuscript. He also provided me with invaluable assistance in other aspects of my research on the Nahuas of Guerrero. My immediate family deserves special mention, especially my wife, Catherine Foy-Schryer, who put up with my long absences; an expert in communication, she provided useful advice about how to develop a style of writing for a wider set of readers. I am also indebted to my brother Eric and my sister-in-law Eileen Foy for their honest feedback and invaluable criticism in the early stages of my book.

This book would not have come to fruition without Frances Benson, the editorial director of Cornell's ILR Press. Her encouragement and comments kept me on track. I am particularly grateful for the constructive criticism of several anonymous reviewers. The final copyediting was done by John Raymond. His queries and suggestions resulted in a better book.